Children of Death

ROBERT LEO HEILMAN

— A SYLPH MAID BOOK —

© 2019 by Robert Leo Heilman

All rights reserved. No portion of this book may be reproduced in any form without the prior written permission of the publisher. Send inquiries to:

Sylph Maid Books
P.O. Box 932
Myrtle Creek, Oregon U.S.A.
97457
(541) 863-5069

ISBN 978-0-9976049-0-0 (Paperback)
ISBN 978-0-9976049-1-7 (ebook: Kindle edition)
ISBN 978-0-9976049-2-4 (eBook: ePub edition)

Cover and interior design and composition by Judy Waller
Interior illustrations by Judy and John Waller
www.johnandjudywaller.com

Cover image, with permission
Russia Restituenda, 1922
Alphonse Marie Mucha (1860–1939)
Mucha Trust/Bridgeman Images

Printed in the United States of America

Sanftmut macht alle gud.
Gentleness makes everything good.

For Casper and Lucille Heilman
And for my son, my nieces and nephews
and for their children

Acknowledgments

Portions of the Introduction, "What's the Use?" and of Chapter 1, "Into the Unknown," originally appeared in *Oregon Humanities,* published online by Oregon Humanities, Portland, OR, October 2014.

Chapter 4, "Day Trip," originally appeared in *The World Pool, A Literary Variety,* Sylph Maid Books, Myrtle Creek, OR as a portion of "Artless Dodger" ©2016 by Robert Leo Heilman.

A portion of Chapter 8, "Boomers," originally appeared in *The World Pool, A Literary Variety,* Sylph Maid Books, Myrtle Creek, OR as a portion of "Work, Stubbornness and the Sweet Life" ©2016 by Robert Leo Heilman.

Chapter 21, "Letter From Home," is taken from the Letter Archive, Letter #1721, of the Germans from Russia Heritage Society, Bismarck ND, website at www.GRHS.org. Translation by Valentine Wangler ©2015.

Chapter 23, "Children of Death," originally appeared in *Heritage Review,* Spring 2013, published by the Germans from Russia Heritage Society, Bismarck, ND and contains excerpts taken from a letter by Dorothea Eisenbraun Ellwein of Neu Lajunt, Crimea, USSR writing to her sister Rosine in America, March 11, 1928. Dorothea died of starvation in 1934. English translation by Armand and Elaine Bauer. ©1979, *Heritage Review,* Germans from Russia Heritage Society, Bismarck, ND. Translation used by permission.

Contents

Maps ~ xi

Introduction: What's the Use? ~ xiii

Into the Unknown ~ 1

Borders and Boundaries ~ 7

The Great Flight ~ 15

Day Trip ~ 19

Departure ~ 23

Rail Line ~ 27

En Route ~ 31

Boomers ~ 37

Turnover ~ 47

Ave Maria ~ 51

Georg and Kasper's Times ~ 55

Her Days ~ 59

Loss of Rights ~ 65

Potemkin's Steps ~ 71

Children of Death

An Accidental Family ~ 81
The World Ocean ~ 89
New World ~ 97
Russiantown Days ~ 101
Four Funerals and a Wedding ~ 105
The Great War ~ 111
Letter From Home ~ 121
Here and There ~ 123
Children of Death ~ 127
Dirty Thirties ~ 133
Two Wolves ~ 135
Little Schoolhouse on the Prairie ~ 137
Dining With the Devil ~ 141
Prairie Storm ~ 147
Unterweg ~ 149
Winter Flight ~ 153
Grandpa's Farm ~ 161
Courtyard ~ 165

Maps

Alsace, Pfalz, Baden

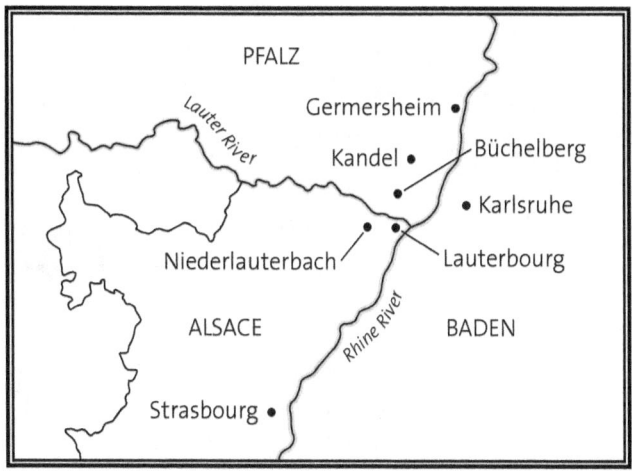

Six German Colonies in Russia

Children of Death

Migration Routes

Introduction: What's the Use?

Sprichworte sind wie Schmettenlinge
Einige werden gefangen, andere fliegen davon.
Proverbs are like butterflies—
Some are caught, others fly away.

Lately, I have been wondering just what the use of it is—not of life itself, which, as long as I have love, is always worth living—but the use of writing a literary work at a time when so very much, the earth itself, seems to be dying. Why bother with history? Why bother at all? I can't bring myself to seriously believe that anything I write will stop the present horrors or prevent the further horrors which are coming any more than they can prevent the horrors of the past. Really, it's all so damned hopeless that I might as well kill, if not myself, at least my scribblings.

In my darker moments I feel so terribly lonely though, and this is the cure, the only cure I know for that: to raise a holler and see if anyone answers. Perhaps in that there may be a measure of solace, for myself and for my readers, that wasn't there before.

It is troubling to me to write about my ancestors, my family, their history, and their world lost to time. They were nineteenth-century Germans and I am not. I could not be a German, or a man of the nineteenth century, any more than a speckled trout could climb a tree. It just isn't in me. I cannot pretend to have much of an understanding of them, beyond what I've learned from books. Book knowledge is better than no knowledge but it's only the uncertain memory of descriptive passages, and not bone-knowledge, which is come by naturally, by living it without ever questioning the how and why of it.

Judging from what little I do know, this unquestioning existence seems enviable to me in many ways. They seem so self-assured, the old ones, though perhaps this is only because they are long dead and so their fate is already complete. When looking backwards things always make more sense than they did at the time when they occurred. You can look back across the centuries and compose a narrative which connects what had seemed, to those living back then, a series of random events. And perhaps this is what appeals to me about their story, just that it is a story. How nice to contemplate that—much tidier than a contemporary story-in-progress such as my own small life.

I am no expert on history, or on culture or philosophy, and so very much of what I understand is just the indistinct shadow of things, an understanding fraught with emotion and not much tempered with reason. Well, I am human. This is really my only qualification for this work and the only basis for anyone to trust what I have to say.

It's true that whenever people look to their

Introduction: What's the Use?

ancestors they are likely to find them both historical and romantic, if not in themselves, then as part of their times.

It is also true that the further back in time you look, the more ancestors you have. They grow in a mathematical progression: two parents, four grandparents, eight great-grandparents, sixteen gr-great-grandparents, thirty-two gr-gr-great-grandparents: sixty-two ancestors in six generations, about 150–200 years. Six more generations, about 350–400 years ago, yields 2,048 ancestors living in the time of the Thirty Years War, plus another 6,152 who came in the centuries after them—8,190 in all; six more generations takes you to the Renaissance and something on the order of 131,000 ancestors, each of whom, you can bet, had an interesting life.

There are people who make a hobby of genealogy, collecting ancestors much like others collect sea shells or postage stamps. In some cases it becomes an obsession, as any hobby can. Sifting through microfilmed files and computerized lists can be great fun, a puzzle more complicated and compelling than a crossword, a diversion that can last for years rather than an hour or two. In the end, however, what accumulates is useless unless put into context, within the framework of history.

They lived; they died. So what?

The uses of history are many, but all those uses come about because it allows understanding, and understanding, in any sense, always comes to us as a story. People need stories as much as they need food and shelter because survival, at its most basic level, requires a sense of identity. As William Kittredge pointed out, a large part of what we struggle with in our lives is the development of a story about ourselves which helps us to understand our world and our role in it, a story to make our lives livable. As significant changes in our understanding come along, the story also must be altered to reflect those changes.

It is an essential yet slippery process, a constant refining of something which is, on one level, the basic knowledge we act upon and yet, on another level, mere play with imagery, a convenient and changeable fiction. Society itself follows this same mythological route to self-awareness which we, as individuals, travel. What makes Russian, German and American cultures distinct from each other is a matter of differing and evolving stories. It is this collective memory of events and their effects, the retelling of the story over the decades and centuries which shapes a people and leads them to healing or to destruction.

      Robert Leo Heilman
      Myrtle Creek, Oregon 2018

Into the Unknown

*Wem'mer so alt wart wie a' Kuh lernt m'r
immer noch ebbs derzue.*
One may be as old as a cow and still learn
something new.

I stood in dappled sunlight inside the ruinous old Catholic cathedral in Selz, Ukraine and asked my translator about the words stenciled in red paint on the limestone wall above where the carved wooden altar had once stood. "All Hail Our Glorious State!" he read, a line from an old Communist hymn, painted there in Stalin's days, back in a time when some people, at least, could still say such things with a straight face.

I looked around me. Large holes in the roof sent shafts of sunlight angling down between the twin rows of columns. Weeds grew between the trash-strewn paving stones inside the abandoned church while outside a half-dozen white goats grazed on the church-yard weeds. Looking around, it was obvious that the state of this church, this town, and this nation were nowhere close to being glorious and hadn't been for a good long time. Turning to the opposite end of the church, I asked about another inscription, a crudely spray-painted graffito located inside the vestibule.

"Well," Sergey sheepishly told me, "basically, what it says is: 'Fuck it all! What's the use? I might as well kill myself.'"

As a child, I came to know that my dad's parents had been born in Russia and that they habitually spoke German. This seemed natural at the time. Old people were, of course, funny-looking and it wasn't surprising that they also spoke oddly, and in my childish awareness, it never occurred to me that people from Russia would speak anything but German.

It wasn't until I was in grammar school that I started my real education in ethnicity, on St. Patrick's Day, when the Mick boys celebrated their Irish heritage by punching any kids who hadn't honored the day by wearing something green. "We're Irish," some O'Malley or Kelly or Moran would announce, "What about you Heilman? Heil Hitler! Heil Heilman! You're a Nazi!"

"But, my grandpa is from Russia," I tried once to explain.

"Russia? Oh, you're a commie then."

"No, we hate the communists," I feebly protested, but, there was just no way to escape from not being Irish.

I remember asking my dad about it once, "Are we Russians or are we Germans?"

"We're Germans," he said after a pause.

"But Grandpa and Grandma came from Russia?"

"Well, they lived there but they're Germans. Heilman is a German name."

"Grandpa talks German," I observed, "He says,

'*Ja, ja, ja*' and you talk to him and Grandma in German."

"Well, yeah, and he speaks Russian too. I learned some Russian from him when I was a kid but later on I found out it was all cuss words. I spoke German when I was little, because that's what they spoke. I learned English in school when I was old enough to go to school. Nowadays I don't speak it so good like I used to."

"But you weren't born in Russia, were you?"

"No, I was born in North Dakota, where grandpa lives. I was born after they moved here to America."

"So, we're not communists, are we?"

"No, of course not—we're Americans."

The post-war 1950s were not an easy time to be proud of our German ancestry, and during those cold-war years any connection at all with Russia could prove not just embarrassing but might actually bring you before a Congressional committee under suspicion of being secretly anti-American. It was all a bit confusing to me and a little mysterious as well. I wondered why my dad didn't want to talk about it.

I remember my grandmother, Marie Eve, trying to explain to me about what had happened to everyone back in the Old World. I must have asked her about our family's connection to Russia. All I recall from that conversation was her attempt to sum up the times of trouble. "The Bolsheviks came and took everything," she told me, "They killed the cows." As a child I pondered that one and felt sorry for the poor cows, who were, I knew, large and dirty but also kindly and harmless. It would take real cruelty, I thought, to kill a poor defenseless cow. I didn't realize that, in the USSR during the early twentieth century, to kill a family's milk cow was a potential death sentence for the entire household. Years later one of my dad's brothers told me that he'd asked Opa Lorenz about family members left behind in Russia. *"Alle veloren; alle gestorben,"* he'd replied: "All lost; all dead."

Opa Lorenz died of heart disease in 1960 at the age of seventy-four, when I was eight years old, and my dad died six years later of a heart attack when he was forty-six years old and I was fourteen.

Over the years I would, from time to time, think of my ancestors and shake my head over their eccentricity—after all, pioneers were supposed to go west across America to farm, not eastward across Europe. What were they thinking? Were they crazy? I could understand why someone would migrate to the United States, but I couldn't imagine why anyone would ever want to move to Russia, a place where, my father assured me, "A human life is worth less than a chicken." And where in Germany did they live before going to Russia? What happened to the Heilmanns who stayed in the Old World? And later: did I have Russian cousins who were taught in school to fear Americans just as I was taught to fear the Russians?

Thirty-five years after my father's death I was working as a freelance writer of magazine articles and one of the publications I wrote for was the Southern Oregon Historical Society's *Table Rock Sentinel*. I had learned to write history, and more importantly, how to research history. One day, while visiting my mother at her home in Los Angeles, I picked up a little book entitled *Ethnic Heritage of North Dakota* and found a small piece in there about the Germans from Russia who, to my surprise, made up about a fifth of the population of that state. It occurred to me that I had the skills to finally learn the answers to my childhood questions.

Borders and Boundaries

A alter Baum lasst sicht nimmi bieje.
An old tree cannot be bent.

In the Advent snows of December 22, 1847 my grandfather's great-grandfather, Johann-Georg Heilmann, jolted along behind a team of horses toward his birthplace. He was 66 years old, though his passport claimed he was 68. He was tall and thin, his black hair turned gray, his brown eyes watching the Imperial Post Road. Behind him was a small village named Elsass, which had been a raw, new sodbuster settlement when he'd arrived there nearly forty years before.

He was about a week into the trip and the covered wagon would creak along for another month and a thousand more miles before he arrived in another small village, Niederlauterbach, Alsace, France. He traveled from Elsass to Alsace, drawn by word of an inheritance. He was traveling toward an unusually historical year, 1848, the year of the Paris Commune and of Karl Marx's Communist Manifesto. His thoughts, however, would have been not on imminent revolutions but on his journey back to the place of his childhood and of the revolution-plagued years of his youth, left behind in 1810 when he came to break sod on the

Children of Death

Nogai Steppe.
It would be impossible to know exactly what the old man was thinking that day out there on the snowy plains. The facts of his days are few and simple: Catholic; born in Niederlauterbach in 1781; named Johann-Georg but called simply, Georg; married in Niederlauterbach to Elisabeth Gutenbacher of Langenkandel in 1803; moved to Langenkandel sometime around 1807; migrated to Ukraine in 1810; Farmer and Carpenter; father of ten with 61 grandchildren; widowed in 1820; remarried sometime between 1821 and 1828 to Magdalena Herth and then again around 1835 to Elisabeth Mock; mayor of Elsass in 1834; died ca. 1848–1851.

His father, Sebastian Heilmann, was a landless laborer as was Johann-Georg until his arrival in *Novaya Russiya*. And though there would have been other reasons for migrating to the Black Sea from Bonaparte's France, the hunger for land was undoubtedly the main reason. The Russian government offered 160 acres of land, freedom of religion, freedom from military conscription, free transportation, and low-interest setup loans to anyone who would settle and farm in the Odessa district—about the same deal (though more generous) which the American government offered his pioneering great-grandchildren seventy-six years later in Dakota Territory.

Really, if you substitute nomadic tribes of Cossacks and Tatars for nomadic tribes of Native Americans, you will have a very good handle on what the German settlement of the Southern Russian steppes involved: wagon trains of immigrant families, temporary mud-brick dugout homes, busting virgin sod with oxen-drawn plows, cholera epidemics, and locust swarms. Elsass in the 1810s might just as well have been Eureka, South Dakota in the 1880s.

The old man's story was one whose outlines would be recognizable two centuries later and halfway around the world, as an American story: a poor man seeking opportunity migrates to a new country, arrives with his young family in a wagon somewhere out on the boundless prairie and, by dint of hard work, creates a richer, more satisfying life homesteading in a pioneer community. Yet his life, lived entirely in Europe, was simply not American.

Labeling his life is a bit complicated, as his life itself was complex. He was a French citizen who became a Russian citizen, yet ethnically he was neither French nor Russian but German. Probably, if he thought of himself as anything other than Catholic, it was perhaps provincially, as an Alsatian, or, more likely, simply as a Niederlauterbacher, a citizen of his birth village. There was, after all, no such nation as Germany in those days, when "Germany" simply meant that part of the world where people spoke German and followed German customs. We've become so tied into the notion of nationality in the past two hundred years that it is hard for us to remember that ethnicity preceded nations, that, for all the ancient "glory that was Rome" the nation of Italy is considerably younger than the United States of America.

It seems odd that Johann-Georg Heilmann left

for France just a week or so before Christmas, a beloved holiday. He was too old and lame to be useful for farm work and his sons were grown men themselves. Certainly, with six of his surviving children married and they with forty-two children of their own already, he had plenty of dear ones who would have kept him noisy company during the holidays. Travel in the hardest part of winter seems unnecessary too. Still, there he was, on December 22, driving across the frozen steppe, about a week out from his home, nearing the Russian border, staring out past a pair of steaming horses' butts as they plodded along.

  He didn't bring any of his family with him for the journey, but he didn't travel alone. Franz Müller, a fellow Alsatian countryman from the neighboring village of Selz, accompanied him and likely provided the team and wagon. So perhaps it was Herr Müller's farming schedule, a need to complete the round-trip journey between the fall *Sauschlacht* butchering and spring planting, that determined the old man's itinerary.

  The English word "homeland," when translated into German, comes out as *heimat,* but the German word has much richer associations. In modern American English "homeland" is a quaint term, useful for talking about far-off strangers—Kurds or Kalahari Bushmen perhaps—or in an obsolete poetic sense when speaking of the past (and lately in the Orwellian New-speak phrase "Homeland Security"), but never for talking about ourselves as contemporary Americans. In the traditional German-Russian dialect one's *heimat* is described by saying *"Wo mei Wiegen stand..."* an idiom that means "Where my cradle stood..." In that winter of 1847–1848, Johann-Georg Heilmann was a man of two homelands: his birthplace in France and his homestead in Russia.

Living as we do now in the first years of the twenty-first century, when we routinely speak of an oxymoronic "global village," it is difficult to understand what home meant not so long ago when virtually everyone lived in real villages and every culture was, by necessity, a local one. *Heimat* perhaps comes closest to our phrase "home town," at least in terms of nostalgic feelings, though for most Americans a home town is a place which has been left behind, whereas for a German, *heimat* is an inescapable fact. Your *heimat* is your daily experienced world, not just the place where you live, but everything and everyone in it. It is defined narrowly in geographic terms but is all-encompassing otherwise, for your *heimat* contains not just people, animals, plants, and objects, but the history, culture, and traditions of that place too—everything for which "there is a time and a purpose." Johann-Georg must have been of two equally emotionally-charged minds while handling the reins that day—one looking forward to the land of the past and one looking back to the land of the present.

On December 23, 1847, Johann-Georg Heilmann crossed the border from Russia at Radzilow and entered the Austrian Empire at Brody. That same day he entered the city of Lemburg, which is nowadays called L'vov, Ukraine.

In 1848, as now, the border between Alsace and Rhineland-Pfalz ran down the center of a small river, the Lauter, whose confluence with the Rhine near Lauterbourg forms the extreme northeastern corner of France. Johann-Georg Heilmann was born and raised in this *Lauterecke* region, in Niederlauterbach, a French village sitting just a short stroll south of the river and a few miles west of Lauterbourg. The land on either side of the river is basically flat—heavily forested for a dozen miles north on the German side and open farming country on the French side.

The border there, and the nations themselves, have shifted over the centuries. Alsace, prior to the Thirty Years War, had been a Bavarian province. The Peace of Westphalia in 1648 ceded control of Alsace to the French. Within the 150 years following that treaty the land changed hands a half-dozen times—French Alsace to Bavarian Elsass and then from Elsass to Alsace, depending on whose army had marched through the region most recently—a cycle which repeated in nearly every generation. In Napoleon's time the Alsatian border shifted north to include most or all of Germersheim district, Rheinland-Pfalz, but after the French Emperor's defeat it returned to the Lauter.

It seems silly to have a river or a creek for a boundary, when a single small cloud can rain on both sides at once. The local people have never cared much for the border. They speak the same Franconian-German dialect on both sides of the river, practice the same customs, and intermarry. The border only matters to their governments, only exists because of a set of written agreements outlining the carefully delineated terms of their nations' mutual distrust. It is fear and distrust which make a river into a boundary rather than a unifying thread—and all because people can't walk on water like ducks or geese.

      Ducks are ducks and geese are geese—neither French nor German—and people are just people, neighbors who look out their windows and see the same sunshine. Only national governments are foolish enough to insist that whether someone lives on one side of a river or on the other side is important. It seems that ducks and geese are wiser.

The Great Flight

Da kamen die stolzen Franzosen,
Wir Deutschen, wir fürchten uns nicht.
Ei, wir stehen so fest wie die Mauren
Wir wanken und weichen keinen Shritt.

Then came the haughty Frenchmen,
We Germans, we do not fear them.
Oh, we stand fast like walls,
We won't waver or retreat a step.

As a twelve-year-old child, Johann-Georg Heilmann may have been part of a flood of refugees who fled across the icy Rhine River from Alsace to Baden. He and his family had the misfortune to be ethnically German and living in Niederlauterbach in November of 1793 when the French Revolutionary Army swept through the Lower Rhine cantons and put seventy thousand German-speaking locals to flight. It was genocide—frankly and coldly so.

They don't call those years the "Reign of Terror" for nothing. The king of France was dead, his head chopped off in a town square in Paris, and the country was ruled by something more ruthless and implacable than royalty—a committee of intellectuals. The old monarchy was terrible enough, corrupt from the skin to the marrow of its bones, but at least it had the saving grace of being limited by greed. What came with the French Revolution of 1789 was ideology, a belief in an idea, and there are no limits to the horrors and cruelties that can be inflicted in the name of an ideal, even one so noble-sounding as "Liberty, Equality and Fraternity."

Theories are lovely to think about. They have a beauty which is impossible to find in the real world. Coming upon one is a sudden thrill, like glimpsing a passing stranger and falling briefly in love. For a moment, a single aspect—a gesture, a flash of color, a smile, a word, or a glance—suggests an entire story infinitely more appealing than what ten minutes or ten years of reality could reveal, because reality is never what you thought it would be. It might be better, or it might be worse, but it will never quite match up with the vision.

There are people in this world who love that happy moment more than anything else—more than life itself. Life is awkward, untidy and unsure, but a theory is elegant, neat, and promises certainty. Those who love life cannot be completely seduced by theories even though they may have them and try to use them. But if a theory occurs to someone who fears ambiguity and clings to a new-found theory like a drowning sailor to flotsam, horrible problems can follow.

The Jacobins would have probably ignored the distant border province of Alsace if it hadn't been for the greed of neighboring monarchs. They had enough problems as it was, assassinating each other and sending first one revolutionary leader and then another to the guillotine. But the situation in France was just too tempting for the neighboring kings. England, Spain,

The Great Flight

Austria, and Prussia joined in the Coalition War in the hope of carving up large parts of France among themselves. In the summer of 1793 a joint Austrian and Prussian army "liberated" most of Alsace, leaving a French garrison holed up in Strasbourg, and then went into winter quarters to sit by the fire until spring while the city starved.

It was a good plan, as military plans go, but the Strasbourg garrison was unexpectedly reinforced by new troops and the French Revolutionary Army drove the invaders back across the Rhine. While they were at it, they decided to "make a fricassee of the damned Alsatians who had polluted the fair soil of Alsace" as well. "The only measure to be taken is to guillotine one quarter of the inhabitants of this area, drive out the rest, and confiscate their property," the Jacobin LaCoste wrote to the *Comité* in Paris on November 22, 1793.

The French army swept through northern Alsace and kept right on going, pushing a wave of refugees ahead of them. "Everybody fled, forsaking father, wife, children and all their belongings," according to a contemporary account.

They ran fast and they ran hard and they ran far, crossing the wintry Rhine River into Baden. "The emigration of two-thirds of the inhabitants of the Bas-Rhin has added much to our happiness," a French administrator reported in January 1794.

Day Trip

Auf d'r Erde baue isch, auf dem Himmel trauer isch.
I build on earth, I trust in Heaven.

*O*nce, I was alone in Strasbourg, where the oldest part of the city lies on an island in the Rhine. I'd come by train, as a tourist with time to kill and curiosity to satisfy on a little day trip. At least that's how I explained it to myself later, on the train, after I'd decided to go.

I went, feeling adrift, unsure of who I was or why, worn by weeks of travel in foreign lands, overwhelmed by strange sights and incomprehensible languages and the effort to see and to remember what I saw. I was homesick, tired of my own company, yearning for an end to my sojourn. I went, not knowing what I'd find in the ancient city, vaguely hoping to see some faint trace of my forgotten ancestors, a glimpse into their world.

The island has served as a trading center, administrative capital, and fortress since Roman times. It has endured while the empires which seized and lost it came and went. Plague, famine, and war washed over it repeatedly. Here, I knew, the world had ended many times and been renewed many times.

Children of Death

I came to a cobbled square near the center of the old city, where a lovely Gothic cathedral, built of rose-colored sandstone blocks, rises. Later, I learned that it is 600 years old and took 150 years to build. Despite its massive size and the stubbornness of stone blocks, it does not overwhelm you with unfriendly bulk, but draws you to its warmth and complexity. The intricate details of ornamentation seem natural and perfectly in tune with its towering scale. Like a mountain, the worn building unfolds, playfully revealing itself in the changing sunlight and shadows, in sculpted forms large and small, each part contributing to the whole.

They built lovingly and well, those long-ago people. I was proud of them, proud of their patience, their skill, their sense of proportion, their humble audacity. Some of the builders, at least, were probably Alsatian ancestors of mine, for the further back you trace it, the more ancestors you'll find. It's certain that some of the people whose blood I carry had walked in this square and prayed in this place.

Inside, the cathedral was dark, the walls stained by generations of votive candle smoke, and the feeling of a long continuous human presence was palpable. Some of the tourists seemed oblivious, as though it weren't a church still in use—day trippers dutifully seeing one more sight on a checklist. But most were quiet, aware that they were in a place made holy by unimaginable centuries of human suffering and yearning.

In a little side chapel in the cathedral I found an old wooden pieta, Mary holding the body of her recently crucified Son. I'm not a big fan of Gothic sculpture, with its stiff poses and stylized portraiture, but this one overwhelmed me. The carver had somehow managed to use the restrictive conventions of his time to convey something hauntingly horrible and hauntingly beautiful and utterly human.

The Son was just a scrawny, ugly, broken and mutilated corpse, human in form but without a trace of personality or divinity, only the final impersonal inertness of death.

Her face wore a mother's expression of profound pain, sorrow, regret, and compassion.

The two figures told an old story, one more ancient than the event it portrayed, and one that the carver had surely seen played out in his own time—for only direct experience could inform such masterful work. I'd seen the same tableaux myself, in news footage from Bosnia, Chechnya, Afghanistan, Iraq, and South Viet Nam. The horror and finality of the corpse, the crushing grief, were the same in old black and white photos from my father's war and in video clips from famine-ravaged Sudan, the debris-strewn streets of Belfast, Oklahoma City, and Beijing.

Here, in a side chapel of a sandstone cathedral on an island in the Rhine, there was nothing I could do except to light a brief candle and pray.

Departure

Auswandern isch der halbe Dod.
Emmigration is a half-death.

Johann-Georg and Elisabeth Heilmann left for Russia in 1810 from Elisabeth's birthplace, a town that is now known as Kandel, Rheinland-Pfalz, Germany. Back then it was called "Langenkandel," an Alsatian town located about twenty miles north of her husband's birthplace, Niederlauterbach, Alsace. They'd only been living there for about two years, probably with her parents. About the only record of their stay in Kandel is the baptisms of twin sons, Johannes and Johann Sebastian, in February of 1808. As a landless carpenter, he was likely forced to leave his birth village to find work living near his wife's family.

Few people leave their homes because they think it might be fun to do so, or because they seek a challenge. Human nature is such that there must be both a prodding at home and an enticement from elsewhere before any mass migration can take place. The people of Alsace back in the first decade of the nineteenth century had both Napoleonic poverty at home and an Imperial enticement from abroad: Czar Alexander I's 1804 Manifesto of Invitation.

Children of Death

Alexander's grandmother, Catherine the Great, was a German princess who came to the throne by marriage and then to command following the assassination of her husband, Czar Peter III, in 1762. It was Catherine who opened land along the Volga River for settlement by German farmers in 1762 and 1763. When *Czaritsa* Catherine died in 1796, her grandson, Czar Alexander I, inherited an ongoing war against the Ottoman Empire. Russia was pushing the Turks out of Ukraine in order to gain land and an ice-free port on the Black Sea. The fishing village of Hadyi-Bey was chosen as the site of a new major city, Odessa. To feed this new city and build up trade, the local nomadic tribes, Cossacks and Tatars, were forced off the land to accommodate settlers from Western Europe.

Alexander's wife, Maria Luisa, was also a German princess, from the ruling house of Baden, and Alexander, like his grandmother before him, turned to German-speaking lands to seek pioneers. He offered free land, transportation, tax exemptions, low-interest loans, freedom of religion, and exemption from conscription to settlers in *Novaya Rossiya*, "New Russia," as he called it. He sent recruiters to Baden, Alsace, and Rheinland-Pfalz to spread the word and arrange for passports and wagon trains.

The recruiters set up secret meetings because in those days, keeping people from leaving the land was more important than keeping immigrants out of the country. The reasoning was simple: Hungry people work cheap, which increases profits, but people who work cheap go hungry and therefore want to leave, which cannot be allowed because empty villages don't provide army conscripts or pay taxes. When you keep people in misery for a living it's important to keep them from leaving your control.

The first wave left in 1804, roughly eight hundred families totaling about five thousand people. Then, for four years Napoleon's wars and the Russo-Turkish wars slowed the eastward flow down to a trickle. But in 1808, the migrations picked up again and continued through 1811 before slacking off until a brief burst in 1816 and 1817. All told, the offer was enticing enough to send twenty-five hundred families to Ukraine for a fresh start farming the steppe lands near Odessa.

Though the emigrés came from many parts of Germany and from Austria, Switzerland, Sweden, and Poland as well, the majority of the families who packed up and left for the Black Sea steppes near Odessa from 1804 to 1811 came from villages in northern Alsace, southern Pfalz, and western Baden, which were located within forty miles of the confluence of the Rhine River and the Lauter River. Among them were 153 people from Kandel, about seven percent of the town's population.

Three convoys of soon-to-be pioneers from Kandel left in 1808, heading east in big wooden Pfalzer farm wagons of the same design as the Conestoga wagons that the Pennsylvania "Dutch" were building in America. Johann-Georg and Elisabeth Heilmann and their four sons stayed until 1810, perhaps waiting for their twins to grow old enough for the long journey to

Novaya Rossiya. They had nothing left to lose.

Every journey begins with a mixture of excitement and dread. When that journey is undertaken as a migration the first day is especially haunted by loss. For weeks or months before that day all the familiar sights are seen with new eyes as though home itself had suddenly become a foreign place. Logic, with its assurances, is useless at such a time. The heart sees what the mind denies, that an old and dear friend is dying, a friend whom you've loved more deeply than you suspected, a friend who is both yourself and the proof of your having lived and loved.

To leave the place where the bones of your ancestors are part of the soil is terribly hard, an amputation that can sometimes be fatal—for any number of reasons. Homesickness alone can be enough to kill you. People sometimes die from broken hearts. Cut off from the people and the place they knew and loved, they become sad, clinically depressed, overwhelmed by the challenges, and, one way or another, by accident or by losing the will to live, they die.

It takes a long time—usually three generations—to learn enough to survive in a new place, because so much of what you know when you arrive there is useless. Every place has its own possibilities and impossibilities. There are new people and plants and animals and soils and weather and diseases to contend with. You can't rely solely on your traditions in a place where you don't traditionally belong.

Rail Line

Wo nix isch hat d'r Kaiser's recht velora.
Where there's nothing the Emperor has lost his right.

I came to the border at a mountain pass southwest of L'vov, where the Bratislava-Kiev rail line crosses from Slovakia into Ukraine. It was sometime in the blackest soul-searching hours after midnight when the ancient train stopped in the brightly lit middle of nowhere. I stood in the hallway outside my compartment smoking cigarettes with the car steward and staring out the open window at a sterile scar bulldozed down the mountainside: two strips of scalped, naked earth on either side of a tall steel fence flanked by rows of jagged concertina wire and looming stark gray wooden guard towers. The landscape had no beauty or grace. Everything there, where the USSR once met Czechoslovakia, was stripped away, revealing an ominous, crushing, silent, willful presence.

"The border?" I asked, although I knew the answer and didn't expect the steward to understand my question. He nodded, his face half-lit and half-dark in profile, and pointed toward the rear of the train. "Slo-vo-kye-yah," he said, and then toward the locomotive, "Ooh-krahn-nee-yah."

Children of Death

On either side of the fence the land looked the same, and was the same. Though the border itself looked so ugly and forbidding that not even birds would dare to cross it for fear of dropping stone-dead from the sky, I knew that the birds, at least, go freely back and forth, oblivious to whether the land beneath them was full of Slovakian worms or Ukrainian worms.

None of it seemed real, at least not in the same sense that people are real, or trees are real, or, for that matter, that pain is real. It was too indifferent to everything around it to be real. The border, so stark, was an imposition of mind, as abstract and brutal as logic—though made of mute steel and weathered gray wood. Only someone far away from this spot could have issued the cold Euclidean decree which declared a line on a map to be more real than soil, stones, water, and grass—or faith, hope, compassion, and love.

I tried to imagine a purpose for this intimidating artifact, now that it no longer served as the Union of Soviet Socialist Republic's imprisoning fence. I'd seen the rusting, crumbling cities and the railroad-side villages full of impoverished peasants, dressed in homespun, leaning on their wooden rakes, watching their cows and goats graze. I saw nothing on either side of this political demarcation that would tempt anyone to invade either country. Everything, for hundreds of miles all around, speaks only of abject poverty, pathetic bluster, and systemic incompetence. There was no power there worth envying, no wealth worth coveting, no lessons worth knowing except, perhaps, "Don't do what has been done here."

Though the border was absurd, I could not

laugh. It was too tragic for that. It was an inhuman abyss which had swallowed so much that, like a black hole, nothing could escape its density. It sat in brooding oppressive silence and in its presence I couldn't find the strength to speak.

En Route

Das Wagnis isch net immer Spass.
Adventures are not always fun.

From Kandel to Karlsruhe, the capital of Baden, was only a day's journey, but one made longer by its finality. One only needed a letter of recommendation from a local official in the home village to be allowed to go on from Karlsruhe to the Russian consulate in Frankfurt and obtain a passport and transportation to Odessa.

The families arrived with their household goods in a farm wagon or pulling a hand cart. Other than clothes, bedding, pots and pans, sacks of potatoes, and grain for seed, they didn't bring much. The Russian government provided low-cost loans to purchase livestock, building materials, and farming equipment once they'd arrived. Most of what they had—and mostly they hadn't much—was sold before they left.

Johann-Georg and Elisabeth Heilmann made the journey in 1810. Along with their four sons, they brought Katharina Gutenbacher-Brossart, Elisabeth's widowed older sister from Büchelberg, and Katharina's fourteen-year-old daughter, Katharina. It was a long, slow trip, twelve hundred miles and three to four months from start to finish, and the twins, at two years of age, must have been a double handful even with two women and a girl to watch them.

The route of 1809 and 1810 was the northernmost, longest, and most difficult of the three migration routes to Russia. The other two ways passed through the Black Forest to Ulm on the Danube. There, colonists boarded barges, called *Ulmer Schachtels*, "Ulm Crates," and floated down the Danube, either to Vienna and overland from there or all the way to the port of Ismail on the delta near the Black Sea.

But when my ancestors left for the east, Napoleon's armies were at war in Austria, and so the wagons turned north to Frankfurt am Main before heading east through Weimar, Leipzig, Dresden, and L'vov on their way to Radzilow at the Russian border. From Karlsruhe to Radzilow they had to live on what food they'd brought and what they purchased along the way.

There were twenty to thirty families in each transport column, a long line of covered wagons creeping along from post house to post house at about fifteen miles per day, six days per week and resting on Sundays. The colonists walked along beside the wagons most of the time amid the incessant crunch of iron-rimmed wheels, the creaking of axles, the steady clomping of draft horses and oxen. They camped and cooked in the open in all but the worst weather when the women and children crowded into the post-house inns while the men slept under the wagons to guard their belongings.

The travelers had to be wary of the thieves, robbers, and rapists who came to the flow of humanity like anglers to a river. The unfamiliar landscape, dialects, and customs battered the emigrants with a constant sense of their own strangeness, of being in limbo, somehow suspended between a dreamlike past and an uncertain future. They were greeted along the way with smiles of altruism and smiles of avarice. Dulled by the unchanging daily routine of waking and walking, as well as the daily and hourly newness of places, they often had difficulty knowing which smiles to trust.

Every wagon train had its share of illness and accident which forced the sick and injured to stay behind and join another column. They contracted the same diseases that accounted for most of the deaths along the Oregon Trail three decades later and half a world away: typhus, dysentery, and cholera. Babies were born en route and death, especially among the elderly and infants, was common.

Immediately upon crossing the border into Russia, a four-week quarantine was imposed to prevent the introduction of infectious diseases into the empire, but in those days of rudimentary sanitation and folk medicine, the camps themselves were breeding grounds for illness. In 1817, the year the ancestors of my grandmother, Maria Eva Keller, passed through it, the quarantine camp at Ismail on the Danube was hit by a typhus epidemic in which whole families, healthy on arrival, died in confinement. Digging graves for the dead became a source of temporary daily employment for some of the men who remained healthy. Altogether about three thousand immigrants died there that year and others, weakened by illness, died on the road from Ismail to the new colonies.

Children of Death

    The quarantine camps, by all accounts, were crowded. The food was lousy and armed guards prevented anyone from leaving. New wagon trains arrived and settled in for the monotonous wait. Stragglers caught up with their families. The immigrants took an oath of loyalty to the Czar and received their Russian citizenship and some travel-expense money. Eventually they were sorted into new groups of twenty to twenty-five families and led across the steppes by mounted Cossacks.

    The large Pfalzer wagons they'd traveled with to the border were replaced by small and crude ox-drawn carts that had no iron rims, springs, or any metal at all. The lack of steel and iron in these wagons was not due to a lack of blacksmithing skills in Russia. With distances so great in Russia, the roads so primitive, and so much of the land undeveloped in those days, it made sense to use a cart that any peasant could repair with a hatchet and a tree limb if need be, rather than one requiring a skilled craftsman and his forge for repairs. These smaller ox-drawn wagons only held three or four people each and separate wagons carried the immigrants' goods. Caravans carrying twenty-five families numbered up to 120 wagons and stretched out for half a mile or more, jolting along at the rate of ten miles per day for 400 miles down the left bank of the Bug River to Cherson and then on to Odessa.

    The country was open grasslands, rolling plains without trees, and the road was a set of ruts, dusty in the summer heat and a quagmire of mud following summer thunder storms. It was daunting country: arid, sparsely settled and exposed, seemingly endless, and nearly featureless. This final month of walking was the longest of all, made longer by the emptiness inside themselves and surrounding them. This expanse was what they'd come to settle, their new homeland.

The wagons rumbled on, carrying not just some people and their pots and pans, but a heavier burden, a cargo of uncertainty. It was a trek from uncertain fear to uncertain hope. There on the endless dusty track crossing the steppes of Ukraine, caught between the immensity of sky and the limitless earth, between what was and what would be, no one could say which of the twin uncertainties was more painful.

Boomers

D'erste hat Dod; d'zweite hat Not; d'dreite hat Brot.
The first [generation] has death; the second has need;
the third has bread.

The "new" land which my ancestors settled in 1810 was only recently emptied of people. The grasslands they homesteaded were called the Nogai Steppe, named after a nomadic tribe of Tatars, the Nogai Horde, who had been removed during the late eighteenth century by Imperial decree and sent to live in the Caucasus to the east, just as the Sioux tribes of the Dakotas were removed by the American government seventy years later and half a world away.

There is a sort of hierarchy of protection which different sorts of people can count on. The rule is that those who are most like the rulers can count on the best treatment and those who are the least similar to the rulers will always suffer most. Thus, nomads suffer more than farmers and ranchers and they, in turn, have it worse than city dwellers, among whom the poor have it worse than the middle class, who for their part are oppressed more than the wealthy. This holds true across time and across societies whether they be capitalist, socialist, or communist. Basically, the less you need to rely on your government and on corporations for your "daily bread," the more likely you are to be oppressed by them. Rulers have always understood that those who are beholden to you for their basic needs are less likely to give you trouble than those who don't need you. The newly arrived German settlers needed the government's help very much; the Tatars, the traditional residents of that land, had needed no one's help at all.

The officials in Odessa settled the German immigrants according to a plan. The government had purchased land from Russian noblemen and picked places where brand new villages would rise. They were careful to segregate the settlers according to their religious persuasions, each village being either Catholic or Protestant, but only rarely mixing the two in the same village. It was feared that the religious differences and prejudices and old quarrels which had caused so much strife in western and central Europe might destroy the colonies before they could take their permanent hold on the landscape.

Unlike the American west, there was no wandering about in search of claimable land according to individual taste. Instead, the families were assigned to one or another village site and had a fixed share in that village's lands. Just as in Alsace and Rhineland-Pfalz and Baden, the families lived on large house lots in town and farmed the land surrounding them rather than each family living by themselves on their acreage.

The Heilmanns' long trek ended on the former

estate of a Russian noble named Cherbanka, who may never have actually seen his land. It was an estate in name and on paper only, a ten-thousand acre expanse of undeveloped prairie country along the Baraboi River. It was a near wilderness, the home of wolves and great black snakes, nearly treeless, and hot and dry in summer and frozen in winter. The 1811 census lists them as one of sixty-two founding families of the village of Elsass, one of six new villages named Strassburg, Selz, Baden, Kandel, Mannheim, and Elsass, totaling some 449 German Catholic families within what became the Kutschurgan administrative enclave, one of four such pioneer-settlement enclaves in the district of Odessa.

It is difficult to understand just how hard, and disappointing, those first years in *Novaya Rossiya* were. Emigration, the act of leaving, brings feelings of loss and uncertainty; immigration, the acts of entering and settling, adds the stressful confusion of arrival and the hard knocks that are the price of ignorance. The early census records for those settlements repeatedly list former residents as *entlaufen* which means "ran away."

The first order of village business was to hitch a team of oxen to a plow and turn two parallel furrows set one hundred feet apart. This marked the edges of the main street and then more furrows, cut at right angles to the first two, became the house lot lines. These lots, just as in their birthplaces, were about one acre in size, rectangular rather than square, and aligned with their narrower sides toward the street. At first the houses were just small one-room adobe half-dugouts with thatched roofs called *semeljankas,* which served much the same purpose of temporary shelter as the sod houses of America's Great Plains would later. There was little time for building shelter in that first summer. Wells and root cellars needed digging, virgin sod had to be turned, crops planted and harvested, fuel gathered for the winter—all of which required long days of backbreaking labor.

The first census, in August of 1811, shows that Johann-Georg Heilmann's household contained nine people: Johann-Georg and his wife Elisabeth; the four sons they'd brought with them, Peter, Lorenz, Johannes, and Johann-Sebastian; and a new son named Georg, three months old and their first child born in Russia. Living with them as well was Elisabeth's sister, Katharina Gutenbacher-Brossart and Katharina's teen-aged daughter, Katharina Brossart. The oldest son, Peter, was only seven years old, and the family must have relied heavily on the three women for field work as well as in caring for the boys. In those days, when hay and grain were still cut with scythes and cattle were watched over by herders, everyone from children to the elderly had plenty of essential work to get done.

The Czar's help was not as great as the colonists expected. Though the government did provide food and low-cost loans for the first year, building materials and farming equipment were hard to come by. Other than a house and his fields, Johann-Georg's property is listed as three horses, a wagon, and a plow—one of only twenty-six of the old-fashioned single-bottom wooden plows among the village's forty-two farmers. The number of harrows—crude affairs which were made of brush—was ten, leaving one available for every four farmers.

The black virgin soil of the Nogai Steppe was rich but tough to break. The Russian wooden plows required three yokes of oxen to pull and three people to plow and drive the bulls. The efforts of six oxen and three men could only turn about two acres of turf per day, a rate which, given the six-to-ten ratio of plows to farmers, only allowed an average of 1.2 acres of plowing per day on new ground for each farmer during the spring and fall planting seasons.

For the first two years most of the farm work went into carving out communal potato and cabbage patches for household staples and through the first decade each household averaged only about six to nine of their 160-acre entitlements under cultivation. Some of the immigrants had never farmed before and those who had were not used to conditions in Eastern Europe. Through trial and error they learned that rye and spring wheat didn't yield much in their new *heimat*, though winter wheat grew well. It took nearly two decades to break enough sod and to adjust to the local conditions well enough to make grain growing a major part of the local agriculture.

The summers of 1828 and 1829 brought locust hordes, great devouring mile-long clouds of them. The colonists lit fires, banged on kettles, fired guns into the air, and dragged stone threshing rollers over the fields where the insects crawled in layers up to four inches thick.

The colonists called 1833 the "Black Year." The summer of 1832 had been dry and yields were so low that many of the colonists had to purchase seed grain. But the seed never sprouted in 1833. The snowless winter was followed by a dry spring and rainless summer. The air filled with clouds of fine black dust, lifted by the wind from the empty fields. For days on end, the sun moved through the sky as a reddish-orange disk that they could stare at without having to blink. Much of the livestock starved for lack of forage and, faced with starvation themselves and mouths to feed, hundreds of the men left to work as field hands in Poland.

During the early decades roughly every other year brought either a total crop failure or a poor crop. Even in the best years, planting and harvesting were limited by the lack of good farming equipment, the burgeoning population left little grain for export, and, of course, good crop years brought market surpluses and low prices.

I've never met a farmer who will admit to having had a good year. To hear it told, there are bad years and worse years, but never any good ones. It is a worrisome way of getting by, one with no assurances that you've made the right decisions.

Every year is different, every crop dependent on whatever the soil, the weather, the insects, and the buyers might offer. Any year can see the sudden onset of plant and livestock diseases. A dark summer squall may bring hail, flattening the grain in a narrow strip only a few hundred yards wide, leaving a sharp-edged path of destruction that levels one field and leaves another, just a few feet away, untouched.

Any two farmers, given the same set of chances, can make decisions that will bring a decent return to the one and disaster to the other. There is no way to know enough to make a safe decision. Prudence might be rewarded this year, or it might not; following a hunch might save you when others are failing or might plunge your family into generations of poverty while everyone around you prospers.

Farming is as difficult to master as any of the other arts. It requires wholeness of vision and the ability to tolerate uncertainty, as well as courage, patience, discipline, and skill. If only it required an audience instead of a strong back and was performed in ninety minutes instead of from sunup to sundown six days per week for several months, county fair exhibition sheds would be as lavishly decorated as opera houses.

One of the great difficulties in trying to understand the past is that most people just don't work like they used to, performing long, hard hours of grueling stoop labor every day—at least, not in the industrialized nations. Maybe that's a good thing. I can't honestly say that I wish I had the inescapable necessity of working like people did in my grandfather's day. I've done enough manual labor to guess at what it must have been like and can assure you that I'd rather be pushing a computer cursor. And yet there is something to be said for going to bed tired every night and waking up hungry every morning.

"By the sweat of your brow..." Adam was told as he left the Garden. A curse, perhaps, but also a formula for health, as aerobics instructors and cardiac specialists will warn you. My grandfather would have chuckled all winter if someone had told him during some August afternoon harvest-work break that a multi-billion-dollar industry would someday be built by millions of people paying good money for the chance to sweat.

Sickles made of bone and flint have been dug up by archaeologists at sites that date back to Neolithic times. For all those thousands of years, people dreamed of a golden time in the mythic past, when the curse of hard work had yet to be laid on humankind. More recently, since the dawn of the industrial revolution with its mechanical gadgetry, the dream has shifted to the mythic future. It is a dream so old, so deeply embedded in human aspirations that we almost never see it as a dream, but take it for self-evident.

But there is a loss that comes with our gain, one that shows up not just in cardiovascular diseases and diabetes, but in a loss of once-common knowledge, a physical education which brings an outlook and attitude as well. There is, at times, a gratifying simplicity and directness and honesty to manual labor. At the end of the day, the results are self-evident and though your body may feel exhausted, your mind isn't cluttered with frustration or stress.

"*Arbeit macht das Leben suss,*" was a proverb of my sodbusting pioneer ancestors, and one which explains a lot about how they endured so much, so well, for so long. It means "Work makes life sweet."

That's a proverb that is almost incomprehensible here in the United States where manual labor is considered an anachronistic evil. It's not the sort of notion that sells kitchen gadgets or movies or beer—Madison Avenue's version of the sweet life. We are taught to avoid using our strong backs (the supposed sign of a weak mind) and to purchase our leisure by working with the insubstantial, to deal in digits and information. Our system rewards us for doing so but gives us poor health.

Turnover

*Weiverstarbe isch ka Verdarbe, ober wenn d'Ross v'recke
sell isch a' Schrecke.
Women's death is no disaster but when the horse perishes
that's a terror.*

I like to imagine Johann-Georg Heilmann at Christmas time in 1812, well fed and warm and surrounded by family, sitting by the stove while up north the remnants of Napoleon's Grand Army retreat from Moscow. In all probability, he would have known of the invasion, but news of the horrors of the retreat wouldn't have reached him yet. He himself, perhaps, had avoided conscription into that frozen and foodless hell by migrating to Russia and it is possible that some of the men he'd grown up with died in that fruitless campaign.

That same year a cholera epidemic broke out in Odessa. The government banned public meetings, travel between villages, and the sheltering of strangers in an effort to keep the disease from spreading to the outlying colonies. Nevertheless, a household in the village of Baden came down with the disease. The house was put under quarantine and the entire household, except for one twelve-year-old serving girl, died within its walls.

The turnover of population in the earliest

Children of Death

years after settlement was so high that the original census of 1811 had to be updated in 1816. Between 1811 and 1816, eight of the sixty-two families in the new village of Elsass along with three single men—roughly thirteen percent of the households—gave up and left. Two of those families and one bachelor moved to Odessa, two more families returned to Western Europe legally, and three other families and two bachelors simply "ran away" without obtaining a passport, presumably returning to their birth villages. In addition, thirty-four infants and children died between August of 1811 and August, 1816.

Among those infant deaths was Johann-Georg and Elisabeth's seventh child in nine years, a daughter named Ottilie, who was born and died in 1812. Six or seven kids a year dying might not seem like much, but in a small village of sixty families, amounting to a little over 300 people, that's a lot of grief. Here in my hometown, Myrtle Creek, Oregon, a town ten times the size of Elsass in those days, that would be equal to sixty or seventy babies and children lost every year. Despite the deaths of the little ones, as well as of four adults, and the loss of the families who ran off, moved on or returned to Western Europe, there was a small gain in the population: from 303 people in 1811 up to 326 in 1816.

Elisabeth Gutenbacher-Heilmann, Johann-Georg's wife, went through at least nine pregnancies during the seventeen years of her marriage, 1803–1820, giving birth to ten known children, three of whom died in infancy. If you work out the arithmetic, she must have been either pregnant or nursing a baby nearly the entire time. Nowadays, in the industrialized nations anyway, it seems incredible, and, given the risks to her health, perhaps even cruel. But back then (as it still is in the poorer countries of the world today) women expected to have a new baby every other year and to lose every third child to infectious disease.

Elisabeth Gutenbacher-Heilmann's last child, Mathias Heilmann, was born and baptized on Thursday, March 22, 1820. Father Oswald Ransch S.J.—the last of the soon-to-be-expelled Jesuit missionary priests to serve the village—was in Elsass on his weekly visit. He'd come to baptize Martin Reis, born two days before, and ended up performing another baptism and the Last Rites for Elisabeth as well. In entering the baptismal record, Father Oswald departed from his usual formula of simply listing both parents followed by the name of their village. *"Georgii Heilmann coloni Alsatientis"* he wrote, and then noted Elisabeth's name followed by *"mortua juxta post partum infantis fluxu sanguinis,"* meaning "she died immediately after birth of infant from flow of blood."

Perhaps, despite the presence of the priest, the midwife first summoned a pious old woman to the house to bless the mother by whispering a brauchen prayer over her three times while making the sign of the cross:

"Es bluhen drei Lilien auf Gottes Hand:
Die eiene isch Gottes Mut,
Die andere isch Gottes Blut,
Die dritte isch Gottes Will'—

Children of Death

Herzgeblut, isch sag dir, steh still !"

"Three lilies grow from God's hand:
The one is God's courage;
The other is God's blood;
The third is God's will—
Heart's blood, I tell you, stay still!"

Ave Maria

M'r muss zum Schmid gehe, nit zum Schmittel.
One must go to the smith, not to the smithy.

On a sunny spring afternoon I stood on a low hump of pasture ground at the edge of a dirt-laned village halfway around the world praying and watching three red cows graze the green sloping field, a place of cow shit, brambles, and weeds.

"Hail Mary, full of grace, the Lord is with thee…"

I'd come to see it for myself, even though I knew there would be nothing to see here, that all that remained was the fragmentary knowledge of what used to be. In my mind's eye I could see this small field as if in memory, though I had no memory of this place that I'd never seen before and will likely never see again.

It was not how I had imagined it. Looking at an old plat map before I left home I'd seen a small square shape covered with little pen and ink crosses marking the graveyard. But there were no crosses there because they were all removed and melted down for scrap decades ago. They were made of wrought iron riveted together in ornate forms. I'd seen their like in North Dakota prairie cemeteries dating back to the homesteading days. *"Hier Ruhe In Gott"* they still say,

Children of Death

"Here rests in God," the words hammered out of glowing metal on anvils.

For generations the Swarzenbergers, a family of smiths, made the wrought-iron crosses which stood there marking the final resting places of the village dead. Each cross was as unique and individual as the life it commemorated, the result of a thousand crafted blows that bent and shaped and fused the rigid metal into sinuous curlicues and sunburst rays emanating from a symbol of sacrifice promising eternal salvation.

"Blessed art thou amongst women and blessed is the fruit of thy womb, Jesus..."

For generations my family lived near the smithy, hearing the ringing sound of their neighbors' hammers striking red-hot metal on anvils. From birth, they heard the day-long sound which also rang for them, as natural and unquestioned as the passing of the seasons.

Nobody makes those crosses anymore. No one even knows how. The smithy is gone. I've seen the empty spot where it stood. In the mud-plastered house that my family built live strangers who draw their water from the same old stone-lined well. The people there have no memory of those who fled from here fifty-two years ago. They've never heard their names—Ball, Bader and Birkenstock, Heilmann, Herger and Honnek, Schwarzenberger, Schell and Schwengler, Urich, Wolf and Ziegler.

They shake their heads "No," sigh and hold up empty palms when I ask. They speak a different language, write a different alphabet, sing other songs, pray other prayers, bury their dead in a different place,

Ave Maria

call this village by a different name.

It's not difficult to imagine how it was. Not much has changed except that everyone who lived here is gone, scattered across five continents. This Eastern European steppe was so much like the North Dakota prairie that I felt I'd known this place since childhood. But all I'd really ever known about it, until now, was a few sad words my grandmother once said and what I learned from books.

There was nothing here when my ancestors came and that, too, is easy to picture. I knew what empty grasslands are—whether they're called steppe or prairie or pampas makes no difference. I knew the sweep of storms on rolling prairie, the wind, how small and vulnerable and exposed you can feel, how your thoughts can stray in such a place with nothing to anchor you, how vast and impersonal, how lonely it is. I marveled at the pig-headed courage of the desperate people who dared to settle here, so far away from everyone and everything they'd ever known, turning stones and mud and thatch into sheltering homes.

I'd come hoping to understand it all—the courage and the work, the joy, the suffering and the loss. But here in this cow pasture where their bones lie hidden, unknown and unknowable, I realized that I can never truly understand the meaning of this place, not the who, or the how, or the why of it. I asked myself what if it was me? And I could only try to imagine.

The sense of what was lost came to me as if it were a fog softly creeping, not hard-edged or overwhelming, but slowly and inevitably as a realization that all was truly forgotten here and that what happened means almost nothing to much of anyone nowadays.

    I came all this way to see for myself that there is nothing remaining here to commemorate their lives, and having come, I prayed. In my prayers I spoke to them all, to these dead who weren't allowed to rest in peace—admitting defeat, expressing regret, asking for their help, and promising never to forget.

    "Holy Mary, Mother of God, pray for us sinners, now and at the hour of our death. Amen."

Georg and Kasper's Times

Armut isch net schlimm so lang m'r Geld hat.
Poverty is not so bad as long as one has money.

There is very little that I, or anybody else, knows about Georg Heilmann, the younger. He was born in Elsass in 1811 and lived long enough to be listed in the census of 1881. A bit late in life, in 1843, he married a woman named Barbara Birkenstock who was born in 1825 (give or take a year).

They had at least eleven children: four sons and seven daughters, of whom two sons and four daughters lived to adulthood and married. Their oldest child, Peter, was born in 1841—perhaps out of wedlock. Kasper, my great-grandfather, was born on October 8, 1851. There were four daughters: Magdalena born in 1845, Ottilie in 1858, Philomena in 1862, and Barbara in 1865.

Most of the records of my people were lost, or misplaced, in the turbulent years from 1917 to 1945. What little has come down to us survived out of benign neglect rather than care.

There were five middle-aged Heilmann brothers living in Elsass and the neighboring village of Mannheim in 1852 and their one surviving sister, Katharina, now married to Johannes Welk and living in the nearby village of Selz, as well. Altogether, with the early church records, there are forty-nine known grandchildren born before 1852, but thirteen of them don't appear on the 1852 list and presumably died before reaching adulthood.

It would not be difficult to invent a set of dynamics and circumstances for the six of them. Any family contains enough tension and history to fuel a novel. Most of these six siblings probably got along reasonably well, though there were perhaps some who despised each other, and, of course, at least one peacemaker who tried to keep them all reconciled.

Their children were the last generation of the clan to know each other well enough to feel themselves a family. By the time that their generation had died the great-grandchildren barely recognized their second cousins as members of the same family. The generation after theirs were, for the most part, strangers to each other.

The long "missing" years passed as they should, in peace and with enough prosperity for a few to become wealthy and for most to live out their lives content. Karl Marx and Charles Darwin, revolutions and emancipations, the humming bee-swarm of isms — romanticism, transcendentalism, nihilism, industrialism, colonialism, nationalism, anarcho-syndicalism, socialism, communism, imperialism — nearly everything we regard today as important events and movements during the nineteenth century, reached our people as the faint sound of distant troubles, if at all.

Change in the Kutschurgan villages moved with the steady pace of oxen pulling plows. The steamship, locomotive, and the telegraph transformed the world around them but hardly touched their lives. In distant capitals an international consciousness awakened among artists and intellectuals, but the farmers looked to their *bashtan* gardens, their fields, orchards and vineyards, and the slow, steady increase of *land und geld*.

The early pioneers had left a provincial world where almost no one held any serious allegiance to any place farther than a half-day's walk from their own village. Here, in their new homeland, surrounded by an utterly alien culture, these families grew even more dependent on each other's shared language and customs.

The Black Sea Germans drew on their past. They continued to practice most of the customs and speak the same dialects that they'd brought with them while in the places they'd left, those ways were dying out. By the time of the Iron Chancellor, Otto von Bismarck, and the creation of modern Germany, they were still essentially an eighteenth-century society, looking no further than their own daily-experienced world, their horizon limited to what they could see about them.

In a naive age noted for excessive enthusiasms, they remained pragmatists. It was a time when great plans were hatched for the betterment of mankind and the relentless march of scientific and industrial progress seemed assured of reaching that best of all possible worlds. Yet the German farmers around Odessa kept to a less dramatic approach to the future. They simply worked hard, played heartily, had many children, and steadily acquired every scrap of arable land that they could afford to purchase or lease.

It was, in many ways, a pessimistic culture. Living at the mercy of nature, with its periodic droughts, storms and epidemics and at the mercy of human nature as well, they found little hope that technological and moral progress would overcome these eternal verities. Nothing seemed assured. At best, things might improve over time for themselves and their children, given enough persistence and a little luck, but even that, the only approach that offered hope, might not pay off.

No culture has ever been perfectly adapted to its people, its place and its times. There is a constant tension in even the most placid of eras and most favorable circumstances. The colonists' virtues were also the source of their shortcomings. Their assertiveness often led to aggressiveness, their persistence to stubbornness, their pleasure in gradually increasing prosperity to avarice and ostentation, their deep commitment to their communities and a healthy pride in their individual and collective accomplishments to provincial arrogance.

Her Days

S'isch ka Mudder so arem, ihr gebt ihrem kind warum.
No matter how poor the mother, she keeps her
children warm.

In each household, the mother was always the first to rise and the last to go to bed. By sunrise she'd already started the fire, nursed the baby, made breakfast, and packed a lunch for her husband and the older children to take along with them to the fields. The housework included not only sweeping and cleaning, washing and mending clothes by hand, baking and cooking, but also the farmyard chores of gardening, feeding the chickens and hogs, cleaning stalls and pens.

There was never an idle moment in her day. What time she had to spare between the essential daily chores was spent spinning wool, weaving cloth and baskets, crocheting, knitting, darning, embroidering, making lace, soap and candles. She would not sit without something in her hands, even when taking time to gossip with her neighbors or teaching the younger children their prayers and nursery rhymes.

Of course, she kept the children busy too, giving them tasks suited to their ages. The kids gathered eggs, helped feed and water the animals, weeded and hoed in the gardens, picked berries, gathered and stacked *mischt* and brush for fuel, carded wool, ran errands, and helped to watch their younger brothers and sisters.

There is something magical about women in how they can feed with loaves, and something also about bread that is magic too, and in that act of baking, a small miracle, something more than bacterium farts and gluten. There is something strong and mysterious about the whole process. Growing the wheat is straightforward, certainly—plant a seed and watch it grow. But, how is it that simple, such elemental foods as wheat flour, milk, eggs, salt, butter and a bit of yeast, turn into our daily bread, a sacred gift from God? I've watched the process since I was a child, even baked, but I still find it strange and unlikely that a sticky mass of gluey stuff will fluff up into a warm, light, aromatic life-sustaining food that satisfies the soul as much as it does the belly.

The ancestors too thought of it as a sort of small miracle, or a blessing at least. "Into the holes the baker has baked his soul," they said. The big round loaves were always marked with a Christian cross cut into the top, done in part to allow the bread to expand, but also as a reminder of its sacred nature. The word itself, *brod*, was often used in their colloquialisms as in the Lord's Prayer—to signify the necessities of life.

The old German-Russians were what is called nowadays a patriarchal society, with men holding most of the public economic and social power over their wives. Husbands physically dominated their wives in those times, back when corporal punishment of men, women and children was thought to be essential to maintaining both domestic and civic tranquility. Yet, within her home and her marriage, a wife made most, if not all, of the family's decisions regarding child-rearing, religious practices, meals, clothing and other domestic arrangements.

When we speak (and think) of pioneering in new lands, we nearly always speak of the masculine aspects of migration, picturing a man on horseback or driving a team and wagon, plowing the fields, hunting. What we seldom consider is their poor wives, uprooted from their homes and attempting to make a home in a temporary shack, bearing and raising children and nurturing the family in a new land among strangers. Which role, if either, do you suppose, required the more care, the harder work, the greater courage?

Most men, I find, fear women. They have realized just how tough the "cookie-makers" actually are. The German-Russian dialect, like nearly all other languages, contains many more pejorative words for women than for men. *Hausdrache* (housedragon), *Hex* (witch), *Hur* (whore). Such terms are never needed for those who are not feared.

Life in the villages revolved around a complex set of remarkably stable daily, weekly, monthly, and annual cycles. Everyone had a role to play and everyone stayed busy. Depending on the day of the week, the time of the day, the season, one's age, gender and station in life, one could say with reasonable certainty what anyone in the village was doing in the past, the present, or would likely be doing in the future. Roughly one-third of the population worked the outlying fields from sunrise to sunset, six days of the week eight months per year. The rest—children, women, the elderly, and a sprinkling of shopkeepers and tradesmen—spent their days in towns nearly small enough that a shout could carry from one side to the other.

From spring to the end of the fall, six days of every week, their husbands and sons left the house at first light and worked the fields until twilight. The boys took up the work at ten or eleven years of age and quickly became used to keeping the same pace as their fathers and older brothers. At harvest, when the work load was heaviest, their mothers and sisters also spent the day in the fields, rolling and tying sheaves of grain, raking and pitching hay, loading the wagons, threshing and winnowing the wheat.

Aside from Sunday and the periodic holidays, what leisure time they had came in the evenings when, for a few hours, everyone in the village was present and still awake. The men gathered in their taverns smoking pipes and playing cards; the women gathered in each other's homes to sit and spin, embroider, weave lace and gossip. The teen-aged girls strolled arm-in-arm along the streets, chewing sunflower seeds and passing groups of young men who teased them and flirted with them as they passed.

The young men gathered into small gangs. These *Kameradschaften* were not criminal organizations like the city gangs of today but served much the same purposes, for mutual support and a way to raise a little defiant hell. They competed in *Gassensingen,* street singing, and in pulling pranks on each other, and on the girls and the village adults—mostly to impress the girls. These petty gangs were sanctioned by the adults, most of whom, although they'd complain loudly in public, didn't really mind having a chicken or a watermelon stolen and eaten by the boys from time to time. The *Kameradschaften* were responsible for staging parades, plays and dances during holiday folk festivals, such as Mayday and *Karwe,* a harvest festival.

Men worked hard during the planting, growing, and harvest seasons and at slaughtering time, but hardly worked during the winter months, when they mostly just sat by the stove and tried to stay warm until spring. They, like everyone else in the village bathed once a week, whether they needed it or not, on Saturday night. On Sunday morning they shaved the week's stubble from their faces, put on clean clothes and went to church.

There were no regular police in the villages. Each householder took a turn as a night watchman for the village, a job which usually consisted of sitting up in a tavern all night, smoking a pipe, drinking coffee and schnapps, and waiting for something unusual to happen. A man's pipe was a sign of his status and how large a pipe he smoked was regulated by both custom and law. No one could smoke a pipe that was larger than the mayor's; merchants' and tradesmen's pipes were larger than farmers'; a young single man could only smoke from a pipe smaller than a married householder.

Each village had a Jewish family or two or

three. These Jews ran stores or taverns and were, for the most-part, accepted within the villages. They were treated with a rough sort of tolerance by the German colonists. They were not given the social standing of Christians and were often the object of half-hearted slurs and cruel pranks but were never subjected to the murderous pogroms common in Russia and central and eastern Europe.

Loss of Rights

Und die Welt geht als immer noch fort, im betrug.
And the world still goes always onward, in deceit.

The promises made by Czar Alexander to our people in 1804 were honored until 1871. Throughout Europe and North and South America in those days a new force called "nationalism" was changing how people, and particularly governments, thought of themselves. The industrial revolution, with its locomotives, steamships, and telegraphs had made the world smaller. Large areas such as the United States, the British Empire, and Russia easily maintained contact between their farthest reaches and their capital cities. It was a profound change, linked to the unquestioned belief in the inevitable progress of science and industry.

With news, people, goods, and armies traveling with greater ease, greater control over the everyday lives of distant people came too. Regions such as Italy and Germany, which began the century as a group of independent and often conflicting states, became much larger and more centrally organized. For the first time in history people began to think of themselves not as Scots, Lombards, Bavarians, Odessans, and Texans, but as British, Italians, Germans, Russians and Americans.

Everything was up for grabs. Vast empires could be won and held by those who developed new technologies and were able to use them in an organized way—the tighter the organization, the better the likelihood of gaining dominance over the rest of the world. The old regional differences of culture were seen as an inefficient hindrance to the advancement of not just nations, but of mankind.

In the Russian Empire, as elsewhere, nationalism had a dark side. The very real need to bring their diverse citizens together in a shared sense of identity and purpose quickly turned into an exercise in narcissism. Naturally, Russia, like every nation, saw itself as superior to any other and within the empire, the demand for a nation with "One Czar, one religion, one language" led to intolerance toward any group who didn't fit into the new sense of national character.

There were plenty of targets in Russia. The vast expanse of Europe and Asia ruled by the Czar held Christians, Moslems, Jews, Buddhists and shamanic tribes. Among the Christians were Russian Orthodox, both Reform and Old Believers, Greek Orthodox, Armenian Christians, Protestants, and Roman Catholics. The city of Odessa was home to Turkish, Cossack, Tatar, Ukrainian, Russian, Polish, Greek, Jewish, Gypsy, French and German citizens, and foreign residents, speaking different languages and dialects and clinging to their own cultural and religious traditions.

Along with everybody else who suddenly didn't fit in, the Black Sea German colonists gave and received their share of abuse. Our people were proud of their heritage—often downright arrogant about it.

Loss of Rights

Unlike the local Ukrainian peasants, they had never been owned as serfs and had, in fact, enjoyed privileges unavailable to the native people of the land they'd settled. Other than collecting taxes and requiring public works labor (most of which was done in their own villages anyway), the Russian government had largely allowed them to govern themselves. They were immune from military conscription and could practice their religion freely. They were free to own, buy and sell land, to establish and run their own schools, to try all but the most serious criminal and civil cases in their own courts, and to conduct village business through their local village councils.

The Colonist Codex of 1848, a set of laws which gave them a measure of local autonomy, was repealed in 1871. It was the first in a series of losses. In 1874 they lost their exemption from military service. Three years later, the Colonist Welfare Office, which had helped to establish the colonies, was abolished. In 1881 the schools were placed under the control of the Ministry of Public Enlightenment and Russian language instruction became mandatory. In 1893 the old German village names were officially changed to Russian names—Elsass became known as Scherbanka, Mannheim as Baraboi, Selz became Limanskaya—though, for the next fifty-one years, the local people simply refused to use the new names in any context other than official business in dealing with the government.

The emigration of German-Russians from the Odessa area began at roughly the same time and increased in numbers as the loss of legal privileges piled up. The first serious migrations to North America occurred in 1872 when thirty to forty families from the Protestant Beresan enclave villages of Johanestal, Rohrbach and Worms settled in Sandusky, Ohio. The following year, another fifty-five families from Rorhbach and Worms crossed the Atlantic and settled near Sutton, Nebraska. By 1914 roughly 750,000 Black Sea, Caucasus and Volga German-Russians had left for North and South America.

The Catholic colonists were not, like some of the Protestant sects, religious pacifists. Their anti-military attitude was more pragmatic than idealistic. Having their young men soldiering for the Czar when they should be establishing families and acquiring land simply struck them as unprofitable, dangerous, and therefore stupid. In those days there were still many people alive whose draft-dodging fathers had come to Russia to avoid conscription into Napoleon Bonaparte's Grand Army. They knew, full well, what had become of the German conscripts who'd marched on Moscow in 1812.

During the Crimean War, from 1853 to 1856, the colonists had been compelled to serve as a labor force, hauling supplies to the front, digging trenches and evacuating wounded and sick Russian soldiers, whom they nursed in their homes. The conditions at the front were terrible, not just due to battle, but mostly because of epidemic diseases. The front came home in 1855 when cholera, brought by the soldiers, spread to the villages surrounding Odessa.

The Fourth Russo-Turkish War broke out in 1877 and for the first time, German-Russian conscripts were among the frontline troops. Then, in 1881, Czar

Alexander II was assassinated, a hint of things to come.

Agents for the American railroad companies began showing up in southern Russia in the mid-1870s. Hundreds of millions of dollars had been invested in the headlong rush to build rail lines across the American west. Huge fortunes were being made and lost in a cutthroat competition to obtain empty land and transportation routes running through the middle of nowhere. The only way for the companies to make their investment pay was to find settlers to buy the land and to use the rails to ship their grain and cattle. Each company hired dozens of agents and before long they found that entire villages in the backwaters of Scandinavia and Eastern Europe could be persuaded to migrate.

These immigration recruiters toured the villages armed with magic lanterns, pamphlets and flyers. When the Russian government began arresting agents, they posed as itinerant farm implement salesmen. Secret meetings were held in homes and taverns at night and extravagant claims were made about the easy money to be made working vast open stretches of amazingly fertile soil which awaited them absolutely free through the courtesy of the United States government.

Finally, in 1884, the first Black Sea German Catholic families from Odessa district began migrating to the United States and Canada. Among them was Georg Heilmann, my great-grandfather Kasper Heilmann's cousin, who in the fall of 1885, at the age of 54, left Elsass to settle in Bowdle, near Eureka, South Dakota, in what was then Dakota Territory. Georg's brother, Sebastian, followed in 1886, settling north of Bowdle, near Hague, North Dakota.

The German people may have been the single greatest pioneering people who ever busted sod. The total amount of prairie, steppe or pampas (which are all different names for the same sort of grasslands) that Germans put under the plow in Hungary, Romania, Russia, Central Asia, South America, North America and Australia may never have been matched by speakers of any other language.

You'd never suspect that this was the case if you had only television and movies and novels to judge by, since, here in the United States, the Old West residents depicted in popular literature and film are usually native-born Americans, or Irish, Scots or English, with an occasional Swede, Norwegian or pigtailed Chinaman tossed in for a dash of humor or a spoonful of *schmaltz*. Yet, large numbers of German-speaking farmers settled in the western United States during the nineteenth century and early twentieth century.

Sometimes I think that the German people must be unusually ambitious, adventuresome and hard-working to have spread out so far and to have cultivated so much land so intensively; at other times I suspect that life in Germany must have been overly harsh to have sent so many of its people fleeing to far lands. I suppose both are probably so.

Potemkin's Steps

Mit Zeit kriegscht du vielaicht Geld, ober mit Geld kriegscht du net immer Zeit.
With time you may get money, but with money you might not get time.

Odessa is more than a city for our people, and more than a place. It is an old story, a mystery and a sorrow wrapped in a single word. For most of us, it is all that we know about our family's distant past—"from Odessa." The phrase has a shadowy substance, at once an obscured source and an impenetrable finality, with something of paradise sadly lost in it and of hell narrowly escaped as well.

Odessa, Texas. Odessa, Washington. Odessa, Saskatchewan. The name came here with us, written in Cyrillic on passports, carried in memories, packed away like family bibles in the immigrants' steamer trunks, carried halfway around the globe and then opened in a New World. But even then, at the moment it came here to be given to new hopes, it was a name for a memory.

Hauling the grain by wagon the forty-five miles to Odessa was a major undertaking for the Kutschurganer colonists. The success or failure of an entire year past and the prospects for the coming year lay tied up in grain sacks in the wagon bed. For most of the farmers the annual trip was their only visit to any city and, more often than not among the first generation born in Russia, the longest journey they made in their lifetimes.

It was a frightening place to them, a cosmopolitan city with broad avenues, monuments, parks and ornate buildings two, three and four stories tall. It was crowded with outlandish people: Turks, Jews, Greeks, French, Gypsies, Italians, Africans and Poles, sailors from western Europe, prostitutes and peasants, aristocrats and diplomats, soldiers, merchants, tavern keepers, con artists, gamblers, and pickpockets speaking four dozen different languages.

The grain buyers were set up on the edge of the city and the first stop was to sell the grain and the protective layer of hay that topped the load. The farmers knew how much grain they'd brought to Odessa by volume but they were paid by the weight of the grain. With no scales of their own, they had to accept whatever the grain buyers' scales claimed. Since the same sack of grain might weigh higher or lower from buyer to buyer, the danger of being cheated was very real and the farmers kept a close watch on the dealers and tried their best to keep informed of who was reputed to be honest and who was not.

From the grain market, the farmers, with their silver rubles tucked inside their homespun underwear, went into the city to buy sugar, coffee, salt, tobacco, axle grease, hardware, farm equipment, and whatever small luxuries they could afford. There were open-air market streets for various kinds of goods, where the

Potemkin's Steps

merchants sold their wares from small booths.

Though the merchants were of many nationalities, the German-Russian farmers preferred to deal with Jewish vendors because the Jews spoke Yiddish, a German dialect which made haggling over prices easier for them and, unlike the Russian merchants, they understood the German way of conducting business.

The German homesteaders were slow to reach a deal. They spent a long while dickering over prices and payment terms, agreeing to nothing until everything had been arranged in precise detail. But, once they'd been satisfied, a handshake and their word were as good as, or better than, gold and more reliable than a written contract. Their honesty in business dealings led the Ukrainians to coin the phrase, *"Nejmetzkoje slovo"* which literally translates as "a German word," but means "utterly trustworthy."

The city offered many enticements, but the farmers were habitually cautious, never spending more than a single night in town and only at certain inns that were reputed to be safe. Even there, unless the weather was unusually bad, they slept in their wagons out in the courtyard to guard against theft.

At times, while walking the streets in the older central part of Odessa, it seemed as though nothing has changed. My mind quickly filled the dry fountain and weed-choked garden of Nicholai Gogol's house with running water and bright blooms, plastered and painted the cracked, dingy walls, placed a liveried servant on the broken marble stairs. Coming upon the entryway to

Children of Death

a courtyard, I half-expected a coach and four to rattle across the cobbles. The ornate and crumbling buildings are Parisian in style, but a Paris that doesn't exist, as if Paris had been left as it stood at the outbreak of the First World War and nothing new had been added and everything left to elegant decay.

Standing by a corner kiosk offering American cigarettes and brightly colored packages of condoms, I waited for a break in the teeming traffic. Rusting buses and battered cars belched the fumes of exhausted engines and among them I saw sleek new Mercedes sedans and chrome-spangled Jeep Cherokees. "Mafia" cars, I was told, paid for with Turkish heroin, prostitution, black marketeering, and extortion. No one else could afford them.

The government hadn't met its payroll in six months. Startlingly pretty young women offered themselves on street corners and the city's rising HIV infection rate was out of control. The pensions and savings accounts of the elderly had disappeared in the floodwaters of inflation. College professors played accordion on the sidewalks to feed their families.

"Democracy has allowed us to open our mouths all we want," the joke went, "But now we have nothing to put in them."

The crows called raucously from the shading trees along a boulevard named for the poet Pushkin, who spent two years here in exile from St. Petersburg. Something of the poet's spirit is said to inhabit them, and so they flock more thickly here than elsewhere in the city. The Odessans say it is great good luck when one of Alexander Sergeyevitch's black angels bombards you instead of the sidewalk.

The people of Odessa take great pride in their city and their heritage. They speak of themselves as Odessans rather than as Ukrainians, as citizens of a great city-state much like ancient Athens or of Florence in the time of the Borgias. They say that the women here are the most beautiful in all of Europe—sophisticated, cultured and *tres chic*. Style is important here, and the ideal Odessan style is gracious, artistic, refined, and cosmopolitan.

"At least, with the Communists, everybody had time," the Intourist agent sighed, telling of the "old days" five years ago. "People would visit. We went to concerts and talked about art, about poetry and music. Now, we have no time. The children, they only want to learn to speak English and use computers. They know nothing. They don't care about anything but money. Everyone is too busy now. We must work always, just to survive, and no one has time to talk, to enjoy life."

"Yes," I replied, nodding in sympathy, "the rat race. It's terrible."

"The what?" she asked.

I looked away, embarrassed. Her office needed painting. The scarred wooden desks held no computers, no fax machines, no photocopiers. There was an old manual typewriter, a mechanical adding machine with a handle you must pull, a telephone through which every call had to be placed three or four times before making the right connection. She sat looking at me, her face deeply puzzled.

"We call it the rat race," I finally explained, "We say that no one has time to be human anymore. Instead, we run about like rats, searching for crumbs of bread, trying to get to them quickly, before the other rats find them."

A few blocks from Pushkin's street stood a massive old stone building painted flat black. It is the headquarters for Ukrainian State Security, formerly the offices and prison cells of the KGB and before that of Hitler's Gestapo, Stalin's NKVD, Lenin's GPU and the Czars' Imperial Police. Nearly everyone in the city and the surrounding countryside can tell of relatives who entered that dark building and were never heard from again.

It seemed a corner to avoid. An unlucky shadow stretched from the ugly building, reached across the sidewalk and across the decades into the past and the future. If you must walk in that shade, you pray for protection from that brooding impersonal blackness where even the sun's light is swallowed and cannot escape.

"What can we do?" people asked me. At times it was an earnest question, but mostly, it was a comment, coming at the end of a discussion, when they shrugged and asked, "But, what can we do?"

It never occurred to me, a fortunate son from the Land of the Free, to wonder what if: What if the British had rounded up the signers of the Declaration of

Independence and sent them all to the gallows? What if the best and brightest of each generation since had been systematically crushed? What if America's past was one of centuries-long brutal repression, an unremitting political rape? What could I do then?

The heart of the city lies not in its middle but at the shore, where a lovely park runs along a limestone bluff overlooking the harbor. The economic and cultural and emotional lifeblood of Odessa flows to here and from here, the port which is the reason it exists, and which gives the city its character. The park, a strip of pavement, grass and trees lined with benches, runs for several city blocks between the wide boulevard and the bluff. A broad set of stairs, the Potemkin Steps, leads up from the harbor to a semicircular plaza facing the sea.

There, atop the stairway stands a bronze statue of Duc Armand de Richelieu, the Father of Odessa, standing with his right arm outstretched, pointing toward the Black Sea. In his left hand he carries a rolled-up scroll which is the subject of an old Odessan joke, having to do with the Crimean War. If you stand in the proper spot, slightly behind the statue and to his right, the seaward end of the bronze scroll protrudes at crotch level, looking, for all the world, like a proud-sized whanger. This, the straight-faced locals told me solemnly, is a message for the city's potential enemies to whom their beloved Duc is offering a choice: "The cock, or the sea."

Coming into the park across the Mother-in-law Bridge, I passed the former headquarters for the now-defunct Komsomol, the Young Communist League, and a soprano voice singing an aria reached me. It was a Sunday in May. The song blended seamlessly with the sunshine, the soft salt-air breeze, the greenery and the sparkle of the sea. It was all so natural, so fitting, that, at first, I didn't quite notice the lovely song. It was as if I myself was the source of the music—like the sound of my pleasant mood, emanating from my own heart.

The singing grew louder as I strolled the promenade alongside my interpreter, a witty and cultured young woman half my age whose knowledge of literature and the arts left me feeling oafish and ignorant. The song grew in volume and clarity. I nodded to the smiling couples, young and old, watched the children scampering about, and concluded that the singing must be coming from a boombox near the plaza. At home, the music would be a thumping bass and the staccato rage of ghetto Rap music. Here, instead, was a charming operatic piece, perfectly suited to the moment and the place.

As I entered the plaza, my companion began to tell me about the voice, an opera singer who arrived a year ago from Moscow when her company was disbanded for lack of government funding. A few short blocks away was one of the great opera houses of Europe, being restored after decades of neglect. I looked upward, searching the windows of the old buildings fronting the plaza, guessing that she must be practicing, preparing perhaps for some grand concert to mark the restoration of the old theater.

But the sound was so loud now that I realized that she must be standing out of doors, perhaps on one of the balconies with their elaborate wrought iron railings, or on a marble doorstep. Perhaps she was not practicing after all, but simply serenading the strollers, filling the air with the beauty that this perfect day had made to spill out from her soul.

At last I spotted her, closer than I had imagined, only thirty feet away from the statue of the Duc. I'd expected a healthy beauty dressed in satin and taffeta. I saw, instead, a mousy little woman, prematurely aged, wearing a scarf, a tattered coat and a plain gray cotton dress. She stood erect, her left arm moving in a graceful, perfectly-trained sweeping gesture, her right hand held by her side at breast level clutching a paper begging cup.

"This is how she feeds herself and her mother now," the young woman told me, "There is no work for her. She was here all last winter too, in the snow. It was so cold, so icy, and I worried about her, that she might injure her voice. What would become of her then? What could she do to earn some food if she became ill and lost her voice?"

Everything in me ached to give the singer something to ease her life. But I'd spent the last of my *kupons* at lunch, sitting under a sidewalk awning, while a slatternly madwoman watched me sip my beer, drooled hungrily, staring with fearful, desiring eyes. I gave the empty bottle to the beggar, thinking she wanted it for the fraction of a penny it would bring her by recycling it. To my horror, the grotesque had lunged at the bottle and sucked at it greedily to wet her tongue with the last few sudsy drops.

Now the singer who'd pleased my soul stood a few feet away. It was Sunday and I had no cash. The credit line for the Gold Visa card in my wallet could feed, clothe and shelter this artist and her mother for more than a decade, but it was impossible to use that piece of plastic for cash or anything else that day. There was nothing I could do for her, for myself, for this proud city brought to ruin.

Her voice remained with me, slowly softening as I walked away beneath the shading trees. I could still hear her when I came to the end of the promenade where a bronze bust of Alexander Sergeyevitch Pushkin, the poet, stood amid the waters of a fountain. Someone, I noticed, had cast fresh red roses into the water to honor his memory.

An Accidental Family

G'heirat isch net d'Kappe g'handelt.
Marriage is not a swapping of caps.

My great-grandfather, Kasper Heilmann, died in November 1897 at forty-six years of age. He had brought his family from his birth village, Elsass, to a small hamlet called Stepanoffka, just north of Strassburg sometime around 1888. Available land had become scarce in the original six villages and the grandchildren of the founders of the enclave began buying up land and creating their own new settlements in Odessa district.

What it was that killed him will probably never be known, but, through one of those quirks of documentation, a list of who he left behind and what he had acquired in the way of worldly possessions before leaving this "vale of tears" was recorded with great precision, attested to by a dozen signatures of the proper sort and somehow preserved despite decades of turmoil.

The art of writing was not invented by poets but by accountants. Most of what we have from the ancient world—the cuneiform clay tablets of Sumer and Babylon, the painted papyri of Egypt, and Phoenician pottery scraps inscribed with the oldest known ancestors of our alphabet—are tax lists and inventories, the record of wealth talking to itself rather than the hopes and fears, stories and prayers of their times. The details of financial dealings, in every age, are too boring to remember and too valuable to forget. Like forgotten old knickknacks, they are left to gather dust in the attic of history.

The record of Kasper's estate doesn't say whether he was a good man or a bad man, whether he was loved or despised. The papers don't say whether he treated his neighbors with kindness or indifference, nor what pleasures he took from life or what pains he endured. These things, so important to himself and his family and his village, meant nothing to the government at the time, nor to any government since.

Georg Müller of Mannheim acted as the executor of his estate. Kasper's house in Stepanoffka and his 13.5 acres of land were leased to some other family and the income from this, amounting to about 60 rubles per year, was given to his widow, Ottilie Lehmer-Heilmann, for the benefit of her underage children.

It wasn't much money, nor had Kasper left much behind for her. In his last year of life, the family's income amounted to 46 rubles and 20 kopeks from farming and 120 rubles and 15 kopeks from selling bread. In those days the annual salary for a school teacher ran about 350–500 rubles, so Kasper's 167 rubles and 35 kopeks were less than half of a teacher's wages.

The rental income from the house and land came to less than half of that. Ottilie moved back to

Elsass with the children, too poor to maintain a household, and so the kids were divided up to live among relatives. My grandfather, Lorenz, was eleven years old at the time of his father's death, old enough to do a man's work. He spent his days as an unpaid field hand, receiving room and board but little affection in exchange for laboring from sunup to sundown.

They worked him like a rented mule. Judging by the stories handed down in the family, his relatives seem to have been more stingy than cruel. He often told his children about eating clabber while the family dined on meat. They were people of their time and in those days long hours of mind-numbing stoop labor were everyone's lot. In the cities, children as young as six routinely worked in factories and mills. In the villages the extended childhood called adolescence, which we take for granted, simply didn't exist. Wresting a living from the land was too difficult to allow a strong back to rest.

It was Ottilie's fate to marry twice, and to outlive both of her husbands. Each time she became her husband's second wife and took on stepchildren to raise in addition to the children she bore with both husbands. All told, she had at least four stepchildren and eight or more of her own to care for during her life.

Sometime around 1900 or so she married August Hoffart, a widower from Mannheim, whose wife, Margaretha Volk, had died and left him with four children whom he'd fathered and a stepchild from her previous marriage to Anton Geilfus. By then, Kasper

Heilmann's three oldest children, Ottilie's stepchildren, had married and so the new household consisted of Kasper and Ottilie Lehmer-Heilmann-Hoffart's four surviving younger children and August and Margaretha Volk-Geilfus-Hoffart's five kids.

It was not exactly what many people nowadays like to think of as a "traditional family," though it was not all that unusual back in those days of accident and incurable diseases, when "until death do us part" often meant a matter of ten years or less. Kasper Heilmann and his second wife, Ottilie, each married twice. So did August Hoffart, and his first wife, Margaretha Volk. It was a complicated set of relationships, the make-do result of five marriages and four deaths among six adults. Lorenz became part of an accidental family, with his three sisters and a brother, two half-sisters and a half-brother, two stepsisters and three stepbrothers, altogether eleven more-or-less siblings, the children of six parents, brought more-or-less together by a need to survive. It was not so much death itself which threatened them, but the poverty brought on by death. Poverty, of course, often leads to death, today as it did back then. More often though, it simply scars everyone it touches.

By the turn of the century, the German villagers of the Ukraine and North Caucasus controlled, through purchase or lease, forty-five percent of all the farm land in the Black Sea region. The six original Kutschurganer villages alone had established twenty-six new daughter colonies, ranging in size from small *khutors* with three or four families to full-blown villages with thousands of acres under cultivation. Despite the flow of thousands of emigrants to North and South America, the price of land kept rising and the descendants of the pioneers were forced to look farther away for affordable farm land.

In 1904 August Hoffart left Mannheim to try his hand at farming in western Kazakhstan, settling in a village named Lublitzki near the city of Kustanai. Located in northwestern Kazakhstan, a little east of the Ural Mountains and just south of Siberia proper, it was an isolated spot, afflicted by long winters and a short growing season.

It was a long journey, over 1000 miles east and north of Odessa, to a raw, harsh land. Leaving his *heimat* for a chance at gaining a better life by farming among the Islamic nomads on the edge of Siberia was a desperate act. August had the comfort of other Kutschurganer families who set off to settle there, but the decision to leave could only have been a choosing between two equally certain evils—poverty at home and hardship in a strange land.

The move to Lublitzki seems to have been a chain migration of the Lehmer family. Ottilie and her husband August Hoffart were moving to where her brother Martin Lehmer (who had married Kasper Heilmann's sister Philomena) settled and where, later, her brother Paul Lehmer and his wife Margaret Wolf and Margaret's sister and brother-in-law, Magdalena and Johannes Keller, would also join them.

Lublitzki was grandpa Lorenz's third or fourth home. He was born in Elsass, raised in Stepanoffka, returned to Elsass, and probably lived for a few years in Mannheim before the family moved to Kazakhstan. He never learned to read or to write. Perhaps he went to a small school for a while in Stepanoffka, or the tiny settlement may have been too small for a school.

He learned what was important in those days: to till, plant, harrow and harvest; to raise and butcher chickens, hogs, sheep and cattle; to drive a team of draft horses and to care for them; to build with stones; to speak Russian; to pray; to sing; to quote the old proverbs; how to calculate without pencil or paper the rubles and kopeks he owed and how many were owed to him; how and when and to whom he should tell the truth.

The year 1904 also brought a lesson in what it meant to have lost their hereditary exemption from military service, when the Russo-Japanese War erupted in easternmost Siberia. Soldiers appeared in the village one day and rounded up all the draft-age young men, ordered them to bring a bag of food and then marched them off to the war. Most of them never returned.

The following year, 1905, revolution broke out. It was an abortive revolution, but sudden and violent. In the cities, factory workers struck and demonstrated openly against the government. In the countryside, peasants simply murdered the landowners for whom they sharecropped and burned down their estate houses. It was all over within a few months, crushed by the Czar's government, but Russia's troubles couldn't be shipped off into exile along with the leaders of the revolt. Following the revolution of 1905, the number of people leaving Russia for North and South

America jumped from tens of thousands to hundreds of thousands. Something was in the air—the stench of fear—and with it, a scent of hope from distant lands.

The World Ocean

Liebe un' net habe isch harter as staan grabe.
To love and not have is harder than digging stones.

In 1908 Grandpa Lorenz married his stepsister, Franziska Hoffart. He was all of twenty-two years old and she was probably twenty. It must have been a wedding filled with tension. Lorenz didn't get along with his stepfather well at all and marrying August Hoffart's daughter after eight years of sharing the same house probably didn't exactly endear him to the old man.

Lorenz was tough and stubborn all his life and had a short fuse in his younger days. August was, at least by Lorenz's account, a typical hard-nosed German-Russian father and stepfather—strict and demanding. It's not hard to imagine the wedding feast, with August brooding darkly over his schnapps and Lorenz smiling, outwardly pleasant but ready to throw a few punches if provoked, while his mother and his stepsister/bride keep watchful eyes on their husbands.

The bride and groom must have loved each other very much. It wasn't a typical marriage for those days when the happy couple were often selected by a matchmaker rather than choosing each other. Since they weren't blood relatives, their marriage was certainly legal and step-sibling marriages were not unheard of among their people. Still, it was a match that took some courage on the couple's part, particularly from Franziska.

Judging by the only photograph of the two, taken three or four years later, they were an attractive couple. Dark-haired Lorenz, whose young face strongly resembles two of my brothers, sports a dapper mustache, a fashion that his generation adopted from military life in the Russian Imperial Army. Franziska, her light brown hair pulled back in a bun, is really quite pretty, a petite young woman with a gentle smile. It's hard to say after so many years and with only one photograph to judge by, but they seem happy together and a little proud, with Lorenz perhaps slightly defiant or perhaps just uncomfortable in a suit and Franziska more shy but peaceful-seeming and a touch amused.

The portrait was taken in 1911 or 1912 in a studio in Dickinson, North Dakota. They sit in ornate wooden chairs with their first child, my uncle Phillip, a baby wearing what was probably his baptismal dress, propped up on a high chair between them. My guess is that they sat for the portrait in order to send a copy to their folks in Russia. "We are happy and prosperous here," they seem to convey, "And such a lovely baby, no?"

Lorenz left for America soon after the wedding while Franziska stayed and waited for him to send for her. She was likely pregnant at the time. Lublitzski was a very small village, a raw pioneer backwater hamlet sheltering perhaps a half-dozen families or less. Grandpa probably wasn't interested in spending another long winter cooped up with his combination stepfather/father-in-law.

He was poor, his only income his annual share of the rent on his father's house and land and whatever he could earn as a hired field hand. He was also ripe for conscription, a five-year hitch in those days, something he wanted to avoid, having heard all about the deplorable conditions in the Russian Army during the recent Russo-Japanese War, and people everywhere were saying that the Russian Empire was on its last legs. He'd witnessed some of the strife during the Revolution of 1905 and heard rumors about more of it.

His mother may have arranged the journey, writing to her relatives in Harvey, North Dakota ahead of time — perhaps before the wedding — asking them to sponsor her son. Lorenz also had other relatives living near Harvey, Heilmanns who had left Elsass for Dakota Territory when he was a small child.

Somehow, he got the notion and the money to go to America and instructions on where to go and how to get there. The money didn't amount to much. More important was the knowledge of how to get there. He couldn't write it down, nor could he read signs and maps along the way, so he must have carried it all in his head, a list of destinations, names strange to him: Hamburg, New York, Chicago, and always, at the end, "Harfee, Nord Dagoda." There was one other important name, a town on the border of Russia.

He couldn't obtain a passport, being a draft-dodger, and so he had to cross over a thousand miles of Russia and then disappear. My guess is that he probably passed through Elsass on his way. There was a sort of "underground railroad" in those days leading out of Russia. Those who'd already escaped to North or South America wrote home and provided instructions on the best routes, giving the names of places and of whom to trust on the way, and what price to pay to be led across the border.

He came to a village or a town somewhere, met with the right people, paid his rubles and left at night. There were smugglers along the Russian border in those days, shadow-men who knew of midnight paths leading into and out of Russia. Hundreds of thousands of Russian citizens were leaving the Land of the Czars in the wake of the Russo-Japanese War and the abortive revolution of 1905 and not all of them had the proper papers to do so. For the smugglers, weighing the cost of capture and imprisonment against silver rubles and heirloom jewelry, the business of leading furtive emigrants out of the country and bringing in untaxed goods on the return trip was very good.

Lorenz told his children that he crossed the border at night, along with a group of Jewish families. To avoid detection by the border guards, the smugglers, he said, gave the children something to drink (probably laudanum, a tincture of opium) and he and the other adults each carried an unconscious child out of Russia.

Opa Lorenz made it to Hamburg, Germany. He may have walked much of the way. It's hard to say, so much of the journey was secretive then and forgotten now. He may have followed the Danube to Bucharest or passed through L'vov and then on to either Krakow or Bratislava, crossing the Carpathian Mountains on the way or, still farther north, he may have gone through

Beyelorus and Poland. I know that it was late in 1908 when he left Kazakhstan and the spring of 1909 when he arrived in Hamburg, so at least three months, and possibly four or five months, had passed and he'd traveled over two thousand miles from Central Asia east of the Ural Mountains to the Baltic Sea.

Mountains, valleys and plains, forests, prairies and deserts, rivers and the sea — the earth has only so many forms, endlessly repeated and yet endlessly varied too. In foreign places the general shapes seem familiar, comforting, but you quickly find that you have no names for the particulars. "Some kind of hawk," you tell yourself, "some sort of poplar." But it is not your particular bird, a red-tailed hawk; it is not your well-loved cottonwood tree, known and understood not only as you see it at the moment but as it was and as it will be through time. "Some sort of laborer, some sort of farmer, some sort of teamster, some sort of barmaid..." But they speak a tongue you don't understand, live lives you can only vaguely imagine. "Some sort of church, some sort of school..."

He came to Hamburg, a city of brick and steel, a Germany very different from the place his great-grandfather had passed through heading east one hundred years before. He spoke an old dialect and could not read a word of what the brightly-colored signs offered. Down by the waterfront along the Elbe River, tens of thousands of emigrants gathered in passenger line barracks and flop houses, awaiting the ships. They came from all over central and eastern Europe — Germans, Jews, Slovakian and Polish and Russian people, speaking dozens of languages. Most of

Children of Death

them were poor. For every first class ticket sold, sixty or more traveled steerage.

Lorenz Heilmann crossed the Atlantic aboard the *SS Graf Waldersee,* a passenger steamer of the Hamburg-Amerika Line. The ship's manifest lists his financial assets as $49.50 USD, which, under the immigration laws of 1909, was fifty cents below the minimum amount needed for entry into the U.S. of A. So many of the details of that journey are lost that it is hard to say how he came, whether he had a prepaid ticket or bought one in Hamburg.

I imagine him homesick and worried, lonely in an incredibly crowded and foul smelling ship. Imagine: two thousand immigrants with their seasickness, measles, chickenpox and tuberculosis, the wailing of babies and the cracked voices of toothless old crones. Ten days or more at sea, and not a thing to be done but wait.

I wonder whether he'd ever seen the sea before. He may have been to Odessa at some point in his life and stood looking out over the Black Sea, or his first glimpse may have been of the North Sea near Hamburg. I imagine him sometimes, at the rail of the steamship staring out across the waters and pondering his future and past. That immensity of blue, the World Ocean, would have seemed oddly familiar to him, a farm hand from a land of sky and endless green.

Lorenz arrived in New York on March 9, 1909. If he hadn't heard already, somebody probably told him about that statue of a crowned woman, lifting a torch on an island so close to Ellis Island that you could almost toss a rock from the immigrant barracks and hit it. He waited, stood where he was told to stand and shuffled along in a long line of people.

Somehow, he made it to Harvey. Having spent several months in transit and traveled nearly 12,000 miles to get there, he stayed a month and moved on to Napoleon, North Dakota.

Franziska arrived in America the following year, 1910. She'd made the long journey in the company of her half-brother, Anton Geilfus, and her brother, Alexander Hoffart. The 1910 Census of the United States lists Lorenz and Franziska on a farm in Napoleon where they were living as hired help. The neighboring farm on the list is that of Johannes Jahner, the husband of Johanna Heilmann-Jahner, Lorenz's older half-sister. Aunt Hannah had, no doubt, arranged the situation for them.

The census also shows that a baby had been born to them who had died in infancy.

New World

Alle Anfang isch schwer.
All beginnings are difficult.

The Northern Great Plains were still very much Old West lands in 1909. Horses and wagons were still the major means of traveling and steam-powered tractors were the exception, while farming was mostly done with horse teams. More than that, homesteading was still going on at a furious pace and masses of people were moving from boom to boom in search of a chance to make a living. The more fertile and wetter eastern side of the Dakotas had already been settled by then, but there was still land available in the drier and thin-soiled western parts. Lorenz and Franziska soon left south-central North Dakota for the west side of the state, settling in Dickinson where Lorenz had an aunt, Barbara Heilmann-Stoppler, living.

The prairies and badlands of western North Dakota and eastern Montana were among the last areas of the United States to be distributed under the Homestead Act. There was a good reason that farming came to this region late in the game, even though open-range cattle ranching had been going on there for decades. The light, sandy soils and dry climate made much of the land useless for crops.

Thousands of families filed claims on quarter-section and half-section homesteads which simply couldn't support a farming family. Most of them failed within the first twenty years as the settlers ran up debts on land which, too often, failed to yield a profitable crop of wheat. The better-educated English-speaking homesteaders were the most likely to fail at farming. Many of them had little or no experience in agriculture and too often they relied on books, pamphlets and advertisements which promised "sure fire" scientific and technological methods of raising crops on marginal land.

Among the many ethnic groups who came to western North Dakota—the Norwegians and Swedes, Irish and English, Germans from Germany, American city-dwellers and Negro sharecroppers all hoping for a place of their own—only the people of the eastern European steppes fully understood how to farm the dry prairie country. They brought with them the seeds of Turkey Red hard wheat, a variety which became the seed of choice. They alone were used to the blizzards, droughts and locusts, hail and fire, all the elements of the fickle cycle of bounty and disaster which prairie wheat farming brings.

In many ways, their ignorance of modern farming techniques helped save them. They knew no other way of life and came expecting the same marginal existence which they and their parents and grandparents had endured for a hundred years. Grandpa couldn't read the glowing reports put out by the railroad companies, the textbooks which promised huge yields and certain profit, the advertisements and pamphlets touting the wonders of mechanized farming. He was a pessimist with an extensive traditional knowledge of farming and a deep distrust of the *Mischtgrawlstudent* agronomist. In time, as more and more families failed and government agricultural agents became more common, the rest of the people of the dry lands lost their naiveté and came to the same necessary attitude.

People shape the places where they live, for good or ill, depending on their skill and understanding. But places, if the people stay there long enough, shape the people as well. This is a matter of culture, the developing of a way of living which will allow people to survive in the place where they live. Since every place is unique, ultimately survival requires a unique, locally adapted culture.

Those who survive on the dry-land prairies learn to distrust the "good" years of bountiful harvests and to expect crop failures. They pray for rain—"But, please, Lord, in the right amount and at the right time"—and work hard as if expecting it to come, all the while preparing for drought. *"Beda isch net genung; do brauch ma a mischt,"* is their watchword, "Prayer is not enough; you also need manure"—that, and skillful work, rainfall, and for the hail to fall on someone else's wheat, and no fires or locusts, and for the horses and cattle to stay healthy, and a good price at the grain elevator. And some years that's what actually happens, a very good year which will, perhaps, earn you enough to survive the next bad year or two.

Russiantown Days

Wer nit kann was er wil, muss wollen was er kann.
Who cannot do as he wants, must do as he can.

Opa Lorenz found work as a laborer and settled in the "Russiantown" section of Dickinson, south of the Burlington Northern Railroad tracks and north of the Heart River. He and Franziska settled in what was probably a row of small wooden shacks on S. Main Street, at an address that no longer exists. The place was a few blocks away from St. Joseph's Catholic Church, which was founded in 1903 to serve the town's growing German-Russian population. Franziska was a founding member of the St. Anne's Altar Society, a group of town women who provided flowers, decorations, cleaning, and clean linen altar cloths for the church. A year later, they'd had a second baby and something to write home about and to send a photo to the folks in the old country.

Lorenz worked as a hod carrier for Messer and Renner, stone masons; then as a laborer for the F&P Brickyard; and then as a teamster for Fred Dietz who had a coal delivery business and a contract with Standard Oil to deliver kerosene, oil and gasoline. Though automobiles and trucks were beginning to come into use, and gasoline tractors as well, Lorenz's coal deliveries were made by horse-drawn wagon. Grandpa was a knowledgeable and skilled farmer who had no land of his own but, like all the German-Russians, he had a great love of horses, and took pride in his ability to care for and work a team.

Nearly all the German-Russians in Dickinson came from the Beresan enclave in Russia, a group of villages neighboring the Kutschurgan. There were also Crimean Germans, Volga Germans, Hungarian Germans from the Banat provinces, Romanian Germans from Dobrudscha and Bessarabia, Caucasus Germans and, of course, Germans from Germany. Dickinson's Little Russia was a small closed world, a dozen blocks of wooden shacks and stone houses set between the Burlington Northern tracks and the Heart River, a community with a shared language that set them apart from not only the English-speaking majority but even from other German-speakers. "Rooshuns," they were called, regardless of their ethnicity—strange, clannish folk who dressed in lambskin caps, fleece vests and heavy greatcoats tied at the waist with a length of hemp rope.

Lorenz labored and saved his money against the day when he could purchase some land. Margaret Wolf-Lehmer's sister's family, the Kellers, arrived in Dickinson in 1910. In 1912 his brother, Joachim Heilmann, came bringing his bride, Helena Wentz. In 1914 his uncle, Paul Lehmer, who'd lived in Lublitzki for a while, brought his wife, Margaret Wolf, and their three daughters. A second cousin of his, Elizabeth

Heilmann, married Sebastian Stoltz and they settled in the area. His son, Phillip, was born in 1911, and three more children followed: Helena in 1914, Margaret in 1915, and Anton in 1917.

All-in-all, it sounds like a lovely example of the American Dream playing out: hard work bringing a slow steady progress toward a long-desired goal of a bit of land to call his own—"Young Man Escapes Old World Oppression, Finds Happiness Pioneering in Land of Opportunity." We Americans love these stories, which support all that is best in our mythology. The reality was more complex than that, darker and more sorrowful.

Four Funerals and a Wedding

Umsunscht isch d'r Dod, un d'r koscht noch's Labe.
Death is free of charge and the cost is your life.

The First World War broke out in the summer of 1914 and an intense wave of anti-German sentiment quickly rolled across the United States. Much of this prejudice was generated by the British, who used the invasion of Belgium to launch one of the first modern propaganda campaigns, aimed at drawing the United States into the war in Europe. Accounts of German atrocities circulated in American newspapers along with cartoons of fiendish Huns attacking Belgian nuns. Crude as these efforts seem nowadays, they were highly effective at the time and were given a tremendous boost with the German U-boat sinking of the *Lusitania*.

Prior to 1914, German culture flourished in the United States. Roughly one fifth of the nation's population was of German ancestry, German language newspapers and magazines were common, and many second- and third-generation German immigrant families still spoke German in their homes and among friends. German bands and *biergarten* were popular. Soon, all things however remotely German were suppressed, at first by individual acts of violence and then, following the United States' declaration of war in 1917, by law.

In Dickinson, the *Nord-Dakota Herold,* a German-language paper published by the Catholic diocese of Bismarck, was required to be published in English, making it nearly useless to the immigrants who depended on it for news from the Old World and for locating lost relatives here in the New World. Preachers were forbidden to address their congregations in their mother tongue. In some places a simple street-corner conversation could land you in jail for not speaking to your own family in English.

Ironically, Lorenz found himself registering for the military draft in a country that had no conscription when he left Russia in order to avoid being drafted into the Czar's army.

Lorenz's brother Joachim is listed as "Jachin Heileman" in the 1914 Dickinson City Directory, but by 1918 the listing shows him as "Jas. Heilmoen," so he became a "James" sometime between the outbreak of the war and 1918. In part, his name was difficult for Americans to pronounce and he may have acquired the nickname "Jimmy" quite naturally, but with the war stirring up anti-German feelings, he must have felt safer being known by a common American name than as the obviously alien Joachim.

The shifting fortunes of those times are also reflected in the directory. Many of the names found on the same page as the Heilmann brothers in 1914 are missing from the 1918 edition. Lorenz, listed as "Lawrence" in both editions, shows up as a laborer in 1914 and as a delivery man for Standard Oil Company in

1918; Joachim's occupation in 1914 as a brickmaker for the F&P brickyard, but in 1918 he's simply a laborer. "Laborer," in the Keiter Directory Company's Dickinson City and Stark and Dunn Counties North Dakota Directory, meant a day laborer, someone who picked up what work he could find from day to day.

It may have been sometime around 1914 that Franziska, grandpa's wife, developed a persistent cough. Tuberculosis is a slow disease, often dragging along for over a decade, making the sufferer's lungs less able to supply oxygen. She could have caught it anywhere, in Russia or on the ship to America, or it may have been waiting for her there in Little Russia. It could have come from a cow through bacteria in the milk, or from another person, perhaps from her brother Alexander Hoffart, who also developed it, or she may have passed it on to him.

I'm sure it was worrisome. The disease had a long and fearful and somewhat romantic history in those days. The slow, wasting nature of its course made it an ideal plot device for nineteenth-century novels.

Franziska was about six weeks pregnant with her fourth child in February 1917 when her eldest daughter, Helena, died suddenly of meningitis. Lorenz bought a plot of ground in the cemetery for the three-year-old and a small, child-sized headstone with an inscription in German. It was the first death in the little family since their coming to America. I can imagine the small group at the graveside: Father Wolpers from the church, Lorenz in a brown suit, his tubercular wife dressed in black and coughing into a handkerchief, their son Phillip, age six, and daughter Margaret, a fifteen-month-old toddler. Uncle Jimmy would have been there too, along with his wife, Helena, the little girl's godmother, and their daughters Magdalena, age three, and Frances, twenty-one months old.

Before the year was over, both Franziska Hoffart-Heilman and her sister-in-law, Helena Wentz-Heilman, gave birth to boys. Helena's baby, Johannes, died the day he was born, December 27, 1917. Perhaps Lorenz gave his brother half of the cemetery plot for the baby's burial, or maybe Joachim bought it from him. The same small group gathered at the same spot again.

This time, Franziska held her own eleven-week old son, Anton, as her nephew Johannes was laid to rest near her own daughter. Five weeks later, February 8, 1918, Anton too died. With three babies lost in just under a year—a daughter, a son and a nephew—Lorenz and Franziska must have wondered at the string of calamities.

Franziska's must have been a life of partings, from her mother who died when she was a child, from her home village in the Ukraine to break new sod in Kazakhstan, from her father, from Russia, and from her short-lived infant children. Women in that pioneering time and among her people aged quickly, and for her that death-in-life was accelerated by a disease common among immigrants. She probably found solace in the votive candles and rosaries of her religion. There must have been joy too, as in every life, but poverty, grief and a persistent cough are the only certain facts that remain.

Four Funerals and a Wedding

That fall an epidemic of Spanish influenza swept through North Dakota on its way around the world. For three weeks it terrorized the people of Stark County, and then left as suddenly as it had appeared. Franziska caught the disease and, weakened by her tuberculosis, died on October 28, 1918. According to the Dickinson Press, she was buried in the church cemetery on Tuesday, October 29, 1918.

It was a busy time. About one hundred residents of Stark County, North Dakota, died in the month-long epidemic, among them twenty-five members of St. Joseph's parish, including the pastor, Father Otto Wolpers. No funeral services were held since the church, along with all other public gathering places, was closed. The deaths were followed by a flurry of marriages following Christmas, which marked the end of the Advent season, when marriages were not permitted. On the thirtieth of December, 1918, two months after Franziska's burial, my thirty-two-year-old grandfather married his Aunt Margaret's niece, Maria Eva Keller, age eighteen—my father's mother.

The Great War

Kein Siega ohna Schade.
No victory without sadness.

Just five years after Lorenz Heilmann left Russia the Great War erupted, and for the German-speaking villages of Russia, 1914 marked the start of over forty years of troubles brought on merely by their ethnicity and their status as rural people. While Lorenz made bricks and shoveled coal in North Dakota, his old neighbors and his cousins back in Russia were being drafted into the Russian Army and called up as Army reserves.

The Russian government, in the name of "pan-Slavic unity," had been heavily involved in Balkan politics for decades. The Russian strategy was to support Slavic independence movements in the region in order to eventually establish pro-Russian proxy governments which would be under the control of neither the Turks nor the Austrians. It was simply a continuation of Russia's southwestward expansion which had been going on since the 1700s.

When Austria declared war on Serbia in response to the assassination of Archduke Ferdinand, Russia declared war on Austria in Serbia's defense.

Germany then declared war on Russia in defense of Austria, which brought the French into the war against the Germans and Austrians in defense of the Russians, and the chain of declarations spread so that within a month or so of Austria's invasion of Serbia nearly the entire continent was embroiled.

The Russian Army was far and away the largest military force involved and yet also the most ill-prepared of the major armies in that utterly senseless war. All wars, whether legally and morally justified or not, are, of course, stupid. But this one was even more senseless than most. In many ways this was due to the personal characters of two of the three emperors in the fight, Kaiser Wilhelm II and his cousin, Czar Nicholas II, neither of whom, it seems, was smart enough to figure out how to pour piss out of a boot—even with a spigot on the heel and the instructions on the sole.

The Russian army amounted to some 1.4 million soldiers during peace time and could be inflated to 6.5 million by calling up all of the empire's reservists. Foolishly, the army's leadership refused to adapt their tactics to the developments in firepower which, by 1914, had made massed infantry charges with bayonets obsolete. The Russian army still believed in the efficacy of mounted cavalry bearing lances and sent them galloping forward against entrenched enemy troops who were using rapid-fire artillery and machine guns with predictable results. In the opening months of the war Russian military radio communications often used plain speech, without the use of codes, which gave the Austrians and Germans who dialed in a tremendous advantage.

The Great War

Not that they needed much of an advantage. At the outbreak of the war the German Army supported the best-equipped land force on the continent, with twice the number of field artillery pieces and four times as much ammunition as the Russian army divisions. Similar rates of under-supply in machine guns, rifles, bullets, railway stock, medical care, medicine and even food held across the board. These shortages, in combination with obsolete tactics, led to huge losses of Russian soldiers.

Among the massed millions serving in the Czar's military were hundreds of German-Russian colonists from the Kutschurgan villages. Their names began appearing in the German-language newspapers of the midwestern United States, first as draftees and then, within months, among the dead, wounded, and captured.

North American readers learned of massive Russian losses totaling millions of men and read the accounts with disbelief. "Surely, every man in Russia must be dead or captured by now," one North Dakotan immigrant reader of the *Staats-Anzeiger* scoffed in 1915. But the names of their friends and relatives from the Old Country kept appearing in the village reports at an alarming rate.

With the outbreak of war, the Imperial government in Russia took emergency steps similar to those which were later used in the United States. The Kutschurgan colonists were forbidden to speak German in their own home villages and were forced to contribute goods and services to the war effort—painfully for the farmers, in the form of confiscated horses, wagons and tack. All of the taverns were shut down for the duration of the war—a move that simultaneously cut off one of the government's greatest sources of tax revenue (the vodka tax) and left the colonists thirsty for their schnapps and beer.

By the winter of 1916–17 the Russian Army was on the verge of collapse. The oldest enemies of all armies—typhus, cholera, dysentery, and malnutrition—were killing as many of its soldiers as the enemy. Along with the army, the nation itself was collapsing. Full-scale revolution broke out in the spring of 1917 with the army and navy plagued by mutinies and the Russian parliament, the Duma, seizing control of the government from the Czar. That fall the Duma itself was overpowered by the Bolsheviks, the most powerful of the socialist factions that had led the spring revolt.

It would be hard to imagine a system more at odds with a society than Bolshevism was to the German-Russians. Just about everything the German-Russians lived by was precisely what the revolutionaries targeted for destruction: marriage, family, individuality, religion, tradition and the private ownership of land.

Socialism cloaked itself in science and proposed radical changes based on theoretical assumptions. Unfortunately, theories are only as good as the assumptions which underlie them. In theory, as H. L. Mencken pointed out, roses should make better soup than cabbages do, since roses are more pleasingly fragrant. In theory, people should be happier without competition and conflict, living as a bland cooperative mass. If human societies were made up of undifferentiated masses, like we find in colonies of ants or schools of fish, instead of being more-or-less haphazard collections of individuals with distinct personalities and emotions (as in elephant herds, wolf packs and all simian groups), socialism would be natural.

The revolutionaries, whether nihilists, anarchists, Bolsheviks or socialists, had destruction in mind—a great cleansing by leveling all the structures of society. For many, destruction was an end in itself. There was no place in their plans for the slow, steady peaceful acquisition of *land und geld*. The drama of death and destruction swept aside the notion of life and growth.

The Socialist and Bolshevik revolutionaries were urban people whose theories were based on industrial models. Nowhere in their philosophy did they seriously consider the role of farmers: people who were both laborers and operators. Ironically, the thinkers who idolized the working classes had nothing but disdain for the hardest working class of all, the peasantry.

It was agreed among the revolutionaries that farmers and farmhands were simply too ignorant to know what was best for them and too stubborn (and perhaps too stupid) to accept the necessary changes which would ultimately benefit them. For their own good, the theory went, they'd have to be forced into the coming workers' paradise. It didn't occur to the prognosticators that the industrial workers whom they pitied were, in fact, rural people who'd been forced from their homes into urban wage slavery.

The largest class of victims of the industrial revolution were (and continue to be) country folk. Karl Marx saw clearly the horror of money, how it cheapens and degrades everyone and everything it touches. Yet, he was also an admirer of progress and European peasantry was no source of innovation. The simple desires of country folk, to have a family with a roof over their heads, a bit of land and enough beans for a warm bowl of soup, seemed like too petty a goal for a forward-thinking progressive society. One might romanticize the "simple" rural people, but their social agenda provided no opportunity for a thinker to make a name for himself. Somehow, frugal contentment just didn't require the services of someone who wanted to astound the world by effecting grand plans.

Revolutions, of course, are always the work of the discontented. On the surface this seems simple enough. When people resent injustice, they try to correct it. However, for the majority of revolutionaries, this discontentment has much less to do with unbearable social conditions than with personal discontent. In the name of society, all sorts of personal grudges are settled and personal gains are made. The attraction of a revolution, particularly for its leadership, is not so much the chance to improve the lot of the society at large as the chance to gain personal power which would otherwise be denied to them.

Socialist ideology, in many ways, took on the aspects of a religion, that is, it became a matter of unquestionable faith. Those who cheerfully announced the death of God at the hand of science readily embraced a political, economic and social theory which, despite its claims of logically proved assumptions, was just simplistic wishful thinking. These ideological cloud castles are often very pretty but usually empty inside and offering little in the way of real protection from life's dangers.

The Red October revolution of 1917 was followed by a bitterly fought civil war lasting some four years. The Whites (as the supporters of the monarchy were known), aided by foreign troops from Austria, Britain, France, and the United States, took on the Red Army of the Bolsheviki. In addition, armed bands of brigands roamed the land looting at will. Whites, Reds and the outlaws all confiscated food, horses and wagons wherever they went in order to feed and transport their forces. The Reds, in addition to their military needs, also requisitioned entire crop harvests to feed factory workers in the cities.

In the summer of 1919, encouraged by the killing of the sixteen members of a Bolshevik food-requisitioning squad in one of the nearby Liebental enclave villages, the Kutschurganers rose up against the Bolsheviki forces. Their resistance didn't last long. Within a few weeks Red forces were burning houses and looting farms at will. Brigette Burghardt-Erck of Strassburg described one such incident:

"When I was 19 years old I married a wealthy young man, Johannes Erck, born on 1 January 1860 in Strassburg, resident of Strassburg. He had a very fine farm. We lived together for 38 years, then in the year 1919 on

Children of Death

August 1st there was a rebellion, then the Bolsheviks came and they shot my husband and they set fire to and burned down the entire farmstead and then they tossed my husband into the fire and I was forced to watch until all was ruined."

On August 2, 1919, the Kutschurgan village of Selz came under artillery bombardment from guns mounted on railcars on the railway line in Strassburg, sending the population of three thousand fleeing into the fields and orchards which surrounded the town. The Red troops entered the village where they spent the night raping women and girls whom they'd captured as well as looting houses and burning them to the ground. In the morning eighty-seven captured men from the village were marched to the edge of town and shot along with the village priest. Four of those men survived the massacre.

There is a soul-numbing which comes with the study of the history of the Union of Soviet Socialist Republics. It is a history of suffering on an unimaginable scale. You read the accounts and the austere numbers are just too massive, too impersonal to understand the measure of mass horror. Your hands may stay soft while turning the pages of books, but in reading them, your mind grows thick protective calluses. A single tale can pierce your hide but endlessly multiplied, as you know the reality to have been, you are left with only dismal statistics.

Four years of civil war brought the Soviet Union's agriculture to ruin and, as a result, five million people starved to death before massive shipments of international food aid brought the famine under control in 1922. In late 1921 Lorenz Biegler from Mannheim wrote to the *Staats-Anzeiger*, a German language newspaper in the United States:

"In two provinces, Saratow and Samara, hunger and disease are so bad that whoever is able leaves all behind and flees—flees in all directions to avoid dying from hunger. Whole caravans travel from town to town, consume all that they can get and move on. The evacuated villages also disappear. Yes, this is a punishment from God, whose mill grinds slowly but surely. Germany is calling its subjects back from Russia, so that they do not die from hunger."

Among the famine's victims were my great-grandmother, Otillie Lehmer-Heilmann-Hoffart, age 61, and her two youngest children, Josef and Maria Hoffart. They died of hunger in Kharkov, 1300 miles from Kustanay, in Kazakhstan, where they had been living. They must have passed through Samara and Saratov on the way, and it seems likely that they were trying to reach their relatives in Odessa district but made it no farther than Kharkov, four hundred miles from the Kutschurgan valley.

Letter From Home

Nord-Dakota Herold
Dickinson, North Dakota
9 December 1921

October 25, 1921   Elsass, South Russia

    Praise be to Jesus Christ in your home! Cordial greetings from your brother-in-law Johannes Müller and wife Elisabeth and our children Anna and Colestia. Dear sister Helena and brother-in-law Heilmann, I want you to know that we continue to be healthy. The father and mother and children Regina, Andreas, Rosina Wentz are all alive and they wish you well. Our father did not die, he continues to live. If you would like, you could send father and mother free tickets so they could come to America. The elderly father and mother do not have bread. Here with us there are no potatoes, corn or wheat so we have nothing to eat. Dear brother-in-law Joachim, it is very sad for us! We have no clothing, no bread and we are naked. We feel like we do not want to live. A Pud of wheat costs 70,000 rubels and there is no wheat to buy.
    The letter that Helena sent on September 7

arrived here on October 25. Brother Andreas sent you a few words in a letter. I, your sister Elisabeth ask you, sister Helena, send something to our father and mother. Send clothing or money. Brother Joachim is still single and he should be able to send something, otherwise mother and father will starve. Brother Andreas would also like to come to America but for now he is a soldier. Sister Regina is also sick. Lorenz Schabler continues to be alive but his mother-in-law has died. Dear sister, the time to send items to America has passed. I, Elisabeth will not be sending you a kerchief anymore because I only have one more left.

    I will now close with a cordial greeting and I ask that you reply soon.

    Johannes and Elisabeth Müller

Here and There

Das Pferd, das den Hafer verdient, bekommt ihn nicht.
The horse that earns the oats doesn't get any.

Opa Lorenz finally acquired his own farm in the spring of 1919, a quarter section in Versippi Township near the Green River. There was a total crop failure that year and in the fall my father, Casper, was born. Lorenz and his new wife moved back into town for the winter and he picked up what work he could as a day laborer. When spring arrived, the family moved back out to the farm where Lorenz farmed for forty years, eventually building up his 160 acres to 840 acres.

It must have been difficult at first for a man and his wife to raise and harvest enough wheat to make a go of it. Phillip, the oldest child, was only nine years old in the spring of 1920, his sister Margaret just four. Maria Eva worked in the fields as well as around the home while still caring for her first baby.

It is impossible to farm for a living without doing damage to your body. It is dangerous work. Sometimes that danger is immediate and obvious, the sort of sudden accident that leaves you missing a finger or two. Sometimes the danger is less obvious, cumulative damage that cripples through repetitive motions repeated over years and decades. Forensic anthropologists can tell when examining ancient Roman burials, which skeletons belonged to slaves and peasants and which to the wealthy just by looking for evidence of damaged spines. *"Och, mein greitz!"* Grandpa would exclaim upon rising from a chair, "Oh, my cross!"

And what of his wife? She too did field work, at least early on, until the two oldest boys were grown enough to do a day's work. Much of her labor must have occurred while she was pregnant. In the ten years following my father's birth in 1919, she gave birth to two more sons and two daughters. There would never have been a time without a baby to care for. My uncle told me that Opa Lorenz paid a doctor to attend those births, and that the cost was a chicken and two quarts of milk for the home delivery—a price that the kids were reminded of whenever they got lazy.

Meanwhile, in Russia, the famine of 1921–22 was tamed by foreign aid coming in to the fledgling USSR, much of it from the United States under the direction of Herbert Hoover, as well as from Western Europe and South America. Bishop Josef Kessler, whose Catholic diocese of Tiraspol included the parishes of Odessa district, visited St. Joseph's Church in Dickinson in April of 1922 while on a famine-relief fundraising tour of German-Russian settlements in the United States, raising $14,000 in North Dakota and another $18,000 in Kansas, the equivalent of nearly a half-million dollars in today's U.S. currency.

Lenin, the USSR's leader, finally announced

what came to be called the New Economic Policy, allowing farmers to keep their farms and to sell their surplus food for profit. This return to a private enterprise system for raising food helped, but the amount of food being raised in the Soviet Union still lagged behind pre-World War I production levels, and a crop failure in Ukraine in 1927–28 brought more severe food shortages.

After Lenin's death in 1924, Joseph Stalin came to power and ruled as a dictator until his own death in 1952. It was he who was responsible for the deaths of some eleven million of his own people during the 1920s and thirties, most of which were deaths among farmers.

The Soviet government announced the creation of the First Five-Year Plan in the fall of 1928. It must have seemed like a good idea at the time, although the outcome was disastrous. In an effort to modernize farm production, farms were confiscated, and individual small acreages were combined to form huge collective operations that were supposed to increase grain production for the country and for exporting to Western Europe, thereby generating cash so that the government could buy factory machinery for the USSR's industrial base.

The plan was carried out quickly and brutally. By 1930 some 320,000 farm families had been arrested in a program known as "dekulakization" and sent over the Ural Mountains to Siberia and Central Asia for resisting the loss of their land. Among them many died en route, and on arrival the survivors became slave laborers.

Children of Death

The grand Five-Year scheme was a dismal failure. Unsurprisingly, the farmers who had been forced into collective farming following the seizure of their small acreages were not exactly loyal enthusiastic workers. The modern farm machines which were brought in to work the larger fields often broke down with no one around who knew how to repair them and, being run by people who had never used a tractor before, breakdowns were inevitable.

The government officials tried their best to increase production by treating their workers more and more harshly. To glean a field for a handful of grain or to pick up a potato that fell from a harvest wagon became a crime against the state and grounds for a sentence of ten years to life in the gulag prison system. When this brutality failed to increase food supplies, the officials blamed their failure to achieve their goals on innate stubbornness and chronic untrustworthiness among the villagers.

Children of Death

D' Alta mussa schterba, d' Junga kenna.
The old must die, the young can.

Dear brother-in-law, sister, nephews and nieces and godchild!

God's greetings to you and may the blessings of the loving Savior be with you in all trials...

Through tears I have to write to you. It is now 14 years that the loving God took my husband, father and provider, to Himself. The oldest was nine years old and the youngest seven months. I have 6 children, 5 sons and 1 daughter... Here, in Russia, it is impossible to find work. It has come so far that we will all starve to death. I don't know what will happen. We have bread only for one month, not a day longer.

The elderly and the infants die first, then the men and the children, and finally the women. The ratio of women to men to children who starve to death follows a mathematical progression of one, two, three: for every woman of childbearing age, two men and three children. One plus two plus three makes six: one woman and two men, and three kids. It's as simple as A,B,C and as inexorable as an eclipse.

The pattern is always the same, no matter

where or when or who or even why famine strikes. If a newspaper headline reads, "600,000 Die in Sub-Saharan Famine," then you know that 100,000 women have died, and in the days before they too drew their last breath, each of them watched two men and three children die: grandfathers, fathers, husbands, sons, grandsons, nephews, cousins and grandmothers, mothers, daughters, granddaughters, nieces. Neighbors and friends.

This morning I stayed in bed until 8:00 am. The children were asking, "What's the matter? Arise." But I would rather die than to live. Starvation is a hard death but, if this is God's will, so be it. If you could see, dear sister, how we are, you would be terrified. Oh, it is impossible that we could come across to you. The way is closed. The foreign countries have no mercy on us. We will all perish and are "children of death."

Five million people living in Ukraine starved to death in the famine of 1932–33, that is, roughly speaking, 833,333 women, 1,666,667 men, and 2,500,000 children. It was a deliberate famine, created around conference tables in far-off capitals and targeted at a specific group of people, designed to accomplish a set of predetermined goals. They died from two years of malnutrition followed by starvation. They died from policy and decree, for the sake of ideology and to enhance the political power structure of the USSR.

It was genocide.

They died amidst millions of tons of grain, much of it rotting away in the open, much of it sold to distant nations while they helplessly watched. Well-fed gangs of Party men searched every house in 20,000 villages, probed for buried grain with long steel rods, left with a handful of dried peas after two hours of searching.

Now I would like to thank you for the 24 dollars which you sent to help us in our need. May God reward you for this. It is written, "Verily I say unto you, inasmuch as ye have done it unto one of the least of these, my brethren, ye have done it unto me." May you be softhearted and help us again, not as a gift but as a loan... We are bare and naked. In Russia there is no material, no sugar, no nothing. Russia was the breadroom now it is the emergency room. I would write you a lot more but it is better not to.

In hundreds of villages mobs of women stormed the *kolkhoze* grain sheds, beat the Party men to death with sticks and stones and their bare knuckles and bare feet and obtained food for a day. In the morning armed troops arrived, shot a handful of the boldest, arrested others and their families, and shipped them off to die in the gulags. New Party men took the place of those who'd been killed.

What can we use to buy things? No earnings, great God, what will happen? Fear grips me when I look into the future. No friend in Russia can help. No one can give a drink of water to another.

They ate the dogs first. The cats were harder to catch but they ate them all too. They ate rats, worms, ants and grasshoppers. They ate nettles, roots, tree bark, grass, straw, dry bones, old shoes. Then many hundreds of them ate the dead.

In some places the entire village died, whole families of corpses lying where they fell, on the floor, in bed, on the doorstep, by the hedge in the dooryard.

Children of Death

Days or weeks later, troops gathered the bodies, hauled them to open pits and tossed them in. "Cholera," they were told, "an unfortunate epidemic."

In the end, there wasn't even enough grain left for seed. Three hundred and fifty thousand tons of their confiscated fall harvest had to be given back to the emaciated villagers at spring planting time. With the long winter over and the seed finally arrived, living-dead peasants and their skeletal horses stumbled from their homes and stables and died on their way to the newly green fields of the collective farms, simply dropped in their tracks and never rose.

The harvest was poor... this spring we cannot sow anything should we receive no seed. We could buy seed but there is no money... Last fall we butchered two five-month-old piglets. They had no fat, but it was at least some meat. By now it is all gone. We cannot buy anything. It is out of the question. There is only one month's supply of bread left and nothing else.

The famine didn't care whether it was the hand of God or the hand of Stalin, or both, or neither, whom it served. It didn't matter. It took their lives just the same, 1, 2, 3.

There was the ache at first, and nervousness, a restless compulsion to search for something to quiet the worried belly. The body drew sugars from the liver and spleen then converted body fat. The hunger-ache grew numb. The skin tightened, wrinkled, grew coarse and pebbly over the thin spots on their cheeks, foreheads, elbows, knees and ribs. The gums grew soft, bled from sores, left the teeth loose in their sockets. The breath smelled foul. Sores appeared at the corners of the mouth. Breasts ceased lactating. Pregnancies ended in miscarriage and stillbirth.

Some went mad and turned to murder, killing friends, relatives, their own children. Some were found alive in a house filled with corpses, crawling on all fours, growling like dogs.

Their muscles lost tone, withered. Exhaustion set in, and with it mental and physical lethargy. Their eyes grew large and sunken. Joints swelled, stretching the skin over hands and feet and knees, blisters full of clear watery pus appeared. Nausea and diarrhea came on and the belly ballooned. Their hearts raced and stuttered. The lucky ones fell dead from the simplest exertions—standing, walking, coughing.

Sight grew dim and their eyes stared unmoving, not seeing. Their brains slowed to a crawl, withdrew into themselves, shutting down thought, then awareness, leaving only the brain stem functions of heartbeat and respiration. They lay in comas for a day or two or a week until their hearts finally devoured the last of their bodies' energy.

Please help us, for God's sake. Have mercy on us wretched ones and help us in our need, if you can. We have only need and misery. Oh, if I had wings I would fly to you. In my dreams I am on the ship which will bring us to America and I see you standing on the other side of the ocean, but I wake up and I am all alone.

Dirty Thirties

Bessa an Wurm im Graud wie gor kein Flaasch.
Better a worm in the cabbage than no meat at all.

My father's first glimpse of the Ocean came in 1936, within months of his high school graduation. Casper John Heilman was seventeen then, one of two boys and three girls who matriculated from Versippi High School near Dickinson, North Dakota that year. Dad came of age during the Hard Times. Lorenz Heilmann, my grandfather, lost his farm three times in those years—to drought, locusts, and drought again—and gained it back each time. The bank, having foreclosed, couldn't sell his place because nobody wanted it. The deed was worthless, and so they signed him to a lease, one which allowed him to use a year's worth of payments as a down payment on the repurchase of the farm. Better some kind of income from the property than none at all, the bankers reasoned.

They were legendarily tough years, those "Dirty Thirties." Opa Lorenz was a master of farming and managed to pull a subsistence from the soil even in years when he couldn't make it yield money. A little egg money, a little creamery money and, too often, a total crop failure. Dad's family lived in poverty—rural poverty with always a bite to eat and roof over their heads, but poverty nonetheless.

Nineteen thirty-five was a particularly brutal year, with drought and dust storms bringing on an almost total crop failure. The following spring, 1936, brought an equine encephalitis epidemic which killed off thousands of draft horses throughout the Dakotas. In the summer of 1936 money was in very short supply and "Cap" Heilman joined the Civilian Conservation Corps, a New Deal program for young out-of-work men whom the government put to work doing brush clearing, tree planting and other conservation work. Under the program the boys earned $30.00 per month for the six months of their "hitch" and were given room and board in military camps. Of the $30.00 per month, the government sent $25.00 to their families and the boys got $5.00 for their own use.

My father signed up for the program in Dickinson, North Dakota, was accepted, sent by train to Fort MacArthur in San Pedro, California, and housed in an army barracks atop Point Fermin, a high white bluff overlooking the Catalina Island channel. He'd never seen the ocean before; in fact, he'd never left the state of North Dakota before. He told me once that the rolling swells and waves reminded him of rolling green wheat fields waving in the wind.

Two Wolves

An Wulf kenna an Wulf.
A wolf knows a wolf.

The August, 1939 nonaggression pact between Hitler and Stalin was more like an awkward marriage of convenience than anything else. Neither trusted the other much. They were, in fact, avowed enemies but they were also both pragmatic men, able to see the advantages. Hitler couldn't afford to invade Poland, as he did a week later in September, if that meant risking the very real chance of having to fight the Soviet Union's Red Army as well as the Polish Army. Getting bogged down for several months in the east would allow the western allies too much time to build up their strength. Stalin, of course, had no desire to save Poland but he might be tempted to send his troops there to hold the Germans at bay farther from his borders. Then, once established in the country, he could take advantage of his powerful army's presence to install a communist puppet government in place of the democratic government he'd supposedly come to help.

The Fuehrer shrewdly offered to share Poland with Stalin instead. Why fight each other, when by pledging friendship they could easily crush the Poles and split the territory between them?

The proposal was a cold-blooded piece of treachery, involving massive numbers of people, genocide and the annihilation of a sovereign state. Stalin was impressed and delighted by it. He and Hitler, he reasoned, obviously had much in common. Herr Hitler, apparently, was as ruthless as himself and, like Stalin, a practical man who wouldn't let mere ideology get in the way of his ambition. Of course, the world wasn't big enough for both of them to rule it—eventually it would have to come to war between the two. But, until that inevitable but far-off day, an agreement such as this would serve them both. Stalin believed he understood his fellow totalitarian dictator perfectly.

Hitler also got Stalin to allow the 250,000 ethnic Germans living in Bessarabia, the Soviet land west of the Dniester, to emigrate to Germany. He planned to create *lebensraum,* "room to live," by resettling the Bessarabian Germans in the homes of Jews and Poles driven out of occupied Polish districts annexed to Germany. From the villages of Baden, Kandel, Selz and Strassburg the Kutschurganers could look across the estuary and see how close they were to escaping Comrade Stalin's oppressive thumb. But they lived on the wrong side of the river and remained while their neighbors a quarter-mile to the west packed up their belongings and returned to their *ur-heimat.* To them, after twelve years of living under Josef Stalin's rule, Adolph Hitler looked like a spotless champion.

Little Schoolhouse on the Prairie

Ena, dena, Tintenfass,
gehst en d'Shul un lernscht m'r was.
Kommst m'r heim un kannscht m'r nix,
nehm isch die Rut und fitzle dich.

Ena, dena, inkwell,
go to school and learn something.
If you come home and know nothing,
I'll take the switch and spank you.

After the six months with the CCC Dad returned to North Dakota and spent the next few years doing whatever came to hand, sometimes going out to California to do field work along with his older half-brother Phillip and serving for two years in the North Dakota National Guard.

"I just didn't want to spend the rest of my life staring at a horse's butt," my father explained. "Besides, I knew I'd be poor if I became a farmer. Your grandpa worked hard all his life, from sunup to sundown, and he never had anything to show for it. There's just too many things working against you: the weather, the markets. You can work hard for years and then lose it all in one growing season."

Later, five quarters of study at Dickinson State Teacher's College during 1938 and 1939 earned him a certificate and a job as a twenty-year-old *schulmeister* for

Children of Death

a one-room school in the Copenhagen School District near Flasher, North Dakota.

"Some of those kids were bigger than I was," he told us.

After teaching in Flasher in 1939, Casper taught at another school near Belfield, west of Dickinson. It was during this time that he met my mother, Lucille Holzemer, at a dance. She was teaching in a one-room schoolhouse near Sand Creek at the time. Dad's Koffler cousins lived in the same Slope County township near Amidon, North Dakota, as Lucille's Holzemer family, and the two families attended the White Lake school. With Belfield being thirty-four miles north of Amidon and the Koffler and Holzemer farms within walking distance of each other, it didn't take long for their relationship to lead to marriage.

Mother was nineteen when she left on a train for Los Angeles, where they married in early 1941. Dad went to L.A. ahead of her to find an apartment and some work. After taking odd jobs for a while, he found steady work at Lockheed in Burbank as a lead man building P-38 Lightning fighter planes in a large building that had been, until then, a whiskey distillery.

On December 7 that year, Japan attacked the United States Navy's Pacific Fleet at Pearl Harbor. On December 19, twelve days later, my oldest brother, Jim Heilman, was born. Because he was working in an essential industry and had a wife and son, Cap went on working at Lockheed through most of the war and was finally drafted into the U.S. Army Air Corps in the summer of 1944, when the need for workers who repaired airplanes was greater than the need for those who built new ones. He was trained as an aviation electrical systems repairman and spent the last months of the war in Deming, New Mexico.

Dining With the Devil

Wer mit d' Diefel essa wolla, muss en langa Leffel han.
Who eats with the Devil must have a long spoon.

On June 22, 1941, the Germans invaded the USSR. The Red Army was unprepared and disorganized. German Panzer divisions and motorized infantry raced across hundreds of miles of the summer-dry steppes. Stalin quickly declared all Soviet citizens of German ancestry to be enemies of the state and ordered their immediate exile to Soviet Central Asia and Siberia.

In the Kutschurgan villages, the German settlers were forced to provide labor—hand digging miles of anti-tank trenches and other fortifications—but the blitzkrieg reached Elsass on August 10. It was too quickly done for the Soviet army to round up the colonists and send them off over the Ural Mountains in boxcars. The Red Army retreated and the Kutschurganers welcomed their liberators.

You can see Wehrmacht films of this period showing German troops entering Ukrainian villages where the people greeted them with flowers and wine. These are not staged propaganda shots. It is simply what happened when German troops showed up in villages that had been living under communism for twenty-four years and performing forced hard labor for several weeks under the threat of imminent deportation. They were glad to see German troops in their villages and, for their part, the troops were glad to enter these places where people who spoke their language and practiced their customs welcomed them.

In the twenty years between 1920 and 1940, at least seven members of our Heilmann clan are known to have starved to death. Nine more were abducted by the NKVD in the dead of night and never heard from again. These are known from the accounts of the survivors. In the village of Selz 158 people, nearly all of them men, were arrested and 114 of them were executed during the purge of 1937–1938. This amounted to about four percent of the population. Similar numbers of executions and arrests likely occurred in other Kutschurgan villages and, if so, roughly 500 executions likely took place in those six villages in those two years alone.

The German government ceded Transnistria, the Ukrainian region lying between the Dniester River on the west and the Bug River to the east, to the Romanian government but retained control over the region's ethnic German towns and villages.

The settlers immediately reopened their churches. Altar stones, chalices and vestments were brought out of hidden nooks to serve Catholic missionary priests. Choirs formed to sing the old sacred songs. Masses were held and large numbers of marriages and baptisms took place. The first dark note in these early sunny days was the execution, with the help of local *selbstschutz* militia, of the Jewish families who'd lived among the German farmers for as long as anyone could remember.

It is painful to consider that the local people assisted in the murder of their neighbors. I keep returning to it again and wondering what I myself would have done. Though there's no real way of knowing the answer to that, I fear that I too might have reluctantly done that despicable deed if ordered by the new authorities.

The virulent antisemitism of the Third Reich came as a shock to the Black Sea German farmers. Each of their villages counted two or three, or more, Jewish families, descendants of Yiddish store and tavern keepers who'd set up shop early on in the settlement period. While the German farmers looked down upon their Jews, their antisemitism was relatively mild. There had never been any pogroms among the German-Russians, as there had been among their Ukrainian neighbors. They were fond of playing coarse jokes upon the Jews and viewed them with disdain, but no more so than they did the Ukrainian *muzhiki* they lived among. Some, at least, of the German colonists protested the expulsion of the Jews, but most, it seems, either feared to come into conflict with their liberators, or simply didn't see the loss of a few Jews as worthy of complaint.

The first wave of executions was carried out by Einsatzgruppe 9, an SS squad tasked with "cleansing" the newly occupied region of Jews and communists. It didn't take long for the local German residents to denounce fellow citizens who had served in Soviet government positions of authority, many of whom had used their positions for personal gain. These local communist officials and the obvious Jewish families were quickly forced to dig their own graves. Later, a second SS unit, Sondercommando 6, arrived to seek out hidden Jews—mostly those who were the product of mixed marriages—as part of a mop-up operation.

Two SS headquarters were set up in the Kutschurgan villages, one in Selz covering the four Kurchurgan River towns and their daughter colonies, while Elsass, east of the river, was governed from nearby Mannheim. The German colonists were looked on with disdain by their liberators. They found them too old fashioned, backward and untrustworthy for their modern taste—not at all ideal models of Nazi *über menschen*. Each local headquarters operated without much, if any, supervision. Punishments for infractions, real or imagined, were harsh, consisting of beatings for the most part along with occasional executions for minor offenses. The SS chief in Mannheim became notorious for getting drunk and ordering random beatings of local people.

In 1943 the Third Reich began conscripting men from the villages. Some were already serving as volunteers as interpreters in the Werhmacht and the rest were mustered into the Waffen SS. Altogether, eight of the Kutschurganer Heilmanns soldiered for Germany in WWII—three in the Wehrmacht and five in Waffen SS units. Before the war and in its early stages all SS troops were volunteers, but late in the war draftees were assigned to these units as replacements. Whether voluntarily or not, the Waffen SS recruits all swore the identical oath of personal loyalty to Hitler himself, rather than to the nation: "We swear to you,

Adolf Hitler, loyalty and bravery. We pledge to you, and to the superiors appointed by you, obedience unto death—so help us God."

Mostly, it seems, "unto death" was exactly how long it lasted. Of the eight Heilmanns from Odessa district who served in the German military in WWII, only one is known to have survived the war, two certainly were killed in action, and the other five are presumed to have either died in the war itself or as prisoners of war in Soviet labor camps.

It is tempting to think of these cousins as hapless victims of both Bolshevik oppression and Nazi imperialism. There's certainly an element of truth in that view, since choosing Hitler over Stalin was about like a coyote "choosing" to gnaw its foot off rather than suffering a slow painful death caught in a steel-jawed trap. However, the fact remains that Nazism was a criminal enterprise and that the Wehrmacht and, especially, the SS routinely committed atrocities and participated in genocide.

If our family is any indication, roughly 10% of the total male German-Russian population of Kherson province served in the German forces: about 200 young men of Elsass, 2,000 men from the Kutschurgan villages and *khutors,* 30,000–35,000 Black Sea Germans. Nearly all of them died in the war or as prisoners of war in Soviet labor camps.

Prairie Storm

Dunner wetter noch amol!
Thunder weather yet again!

Prairie, steppe or pampas—it is all the same when you stand there between the sky and a sea of grass. There is something disturbingly menacing about the seeming emptiness of the grasslands. You find yourself exposed to whatever the weather brings: wind, rain, hail, snow or summer's billowing dust. There is no way to hide from its sudden arrival.

Lightning can strike, hail can cut through a wheat field leaving a line of toppled wheat as sharply delineated as a knife cut, a blizzard can come on suddenly and leave you directionless in your own farmyard. It takes a certain courage to live in such places where the land, so beautiful and bountiful, can kill you or someone you love without warning.

And this is true now, more than a century after the settling on the land—back when the white sun-bleached bones of bison still littered the ground. How much more sinister it must have seemed back then. Some of the early homesteaders went mad from loneliness and an inescapable sense of vulnerability.

Seeing this western North Dakota prairie

country today, which contains more places that people have left than ones where some have stayed, it's hard to imagine how lively it was a few decades ago. Though every back road runs past a few collections of old buildings that still stand, most of the farmsteads are traceable only by a clump of poplars planted as windbreaks that shelter no one. Except for an occasional rock foundation, a well, and perhaps a few apple trees gone brushy, you'd never guess that a family's lives were played out there.

The revolution in farming brought on by machinery, chemicals, and hybrids has left the land more productive but with fewer people. My cousin, Ernie Holzemer, farmed about sixteen hundred acres near Amidon, North Dakota, supporting no one but himself, a bachelor, on ten quarter-sections, enough land at the turn of the century to support ten families. This ten-to-one ratio nearly matches the census figures for America as a whole. At one time ninety percent of Americans were rural folk and ten percent lived in cities. Nowadays nine of ten Americans live in cities while only one in ten live in the countryside.

It's hard to imagine how profound a change this really is. In ancient times, decimation, the practice of executing every tenth captive following a victory, was enough to earn an obscure tyrant a place in history. Yet, rural America has lost many times more people than mere decimation would have caused. The cruelest tyrants are abstract forces. Tamerlane, I'm sure, walks around Hell muttering to himself, "Progress... Damn! Why didn't I think of that?"

Unterweg

Bessa gerrant als verbrannt.
Better to flee than to burn.

*T*hey left on a Wednesday morning, March 22, 1944, while Soviet artillery boomed in the distance—the whole village of Elsass, 2,000 or so people in a long line of hastily covered wagons, with their cattle and horses. Elsass was just one village along with five other villages totaling 14,000 people; a small part of a trek involving dozens of *khutors*, villages and towns amounting to 350,000 people.

In the wagons, along with the simple goods they could take along, were the elderly and infants. Small boys rode on the wagon-tongues, while most of the people walked alongside and behind, slowly, tending the herds of horses and cattle.

It's hard to count them all; they won't hold still. Of the Heilmanns, there were twelve households containing seventeen more-or-less families. Counting the dead and disappeared and conscripted, there were 104 members of the clan altogether: half male, half female; half children, half adults. One hundred and four individuals, but eighteen were dead for sure, and nine took a final ride in a Black Maria in the dead of night, and despite the all the earnest prayers and fond hopes were never heard from again. So, seventy-seven were left alive, or alive enough to count as living. But then five were in the German Army: one in the Wehrmacht, and four more in the Waffen SS, two of whom were reported as missing in action "for Fuhrer and Heimat" since October of 1943.

One of them, old Ludwig Heilmann, born in 1861, at 83 the oldest of the clan, didn't make it to Germany. He died somewhere along the way. Three days out, on March 25, 1944, another Ludwig Heilmann was born in the village of Mariental, and his cousin, Julianna, was born six days later in Romania. Barbara Heilmann-Schnellbach, grandpa Lorenz's widowed sister, age fifty-nine, was among them.

For many, their future was running out. Barbara Heilmann-Schnellbach would arrive at a refugee camp in Germany and then disappear from history a few months later. Mathias Heilmann, age thirty-seven, was given German citizenship and then drafted by the Wehrmacht and killed near Krakow, Poland by Christmas of 1944, in the same frozen month in which my father's brother, George Heilman, age twenty-three, spent seventeen days in combat during the Battle of the Bulge. Old Peter Heilmann, seventy years old, was murdered two years later, shot in post-war Germany in a random act of violence. They couldn't hold still, these people, they just kept moving, to the sound of draft horses' hooves, rumbling wagons, creaking axles and the distant thunder of artillery, moving from the past to the future.

They made a choice—capture, exile and a

slave's death at the hands of the Soviets or this long, sad westward walk from home into chaos. They left the land and with it their identity. For 136 years they were just themselves, *unser leit,* "our people." Then, they had little, only memories. Others told them who they were, *Ausländer Deutschen,* Foreign Germans. Others knew them as an issue, a social and logistical problem, as a need for transport, food, clothing and shelter, as a source of labor and, in those final months of a hopeless war, as bodies to throw down before the Soviet cannons and tanks, like futile sandbags before Noah's own high water.

Underway, there was the day to survive, a few more muddy creaking miles to carry the knowledge of what was lost, and then another campfire meal to feed the children.

Winter Flight

Im Krieg wird keiner verschont.
In war no one is spared.

The Kutschurganer refugees had barely begun the long work of settling down in their new homeland, long enough to begin finding housing, some work, and their lost relatives, and to spend their first Christmas in Germany, when the final Soviet offensive reopened along the Vistula River on the night of January 12, 1945.

The Eastern Front collapsed like a house of cards under the weight of the Red Army's 300 divisions of artillery, armor and infantry. Though German military intelligence knew the date and time of the coming offensive, as well as just how many troops they faced, very little was done militarily to prepare for the attack and nothing was done to warn or evacuate the civilians living in the border districts along the Eastern Front. They were living, right up to the arrival of Soviet troops in their villages, under the assurance that new secret weapons and the determination of the Wehrmacht would ensure their safety.

The reality was that Hitler, shaken by the assassination attempt against him the previous summer (and likely suffering from amphetamine-induced psychosis) no longer trusted what his General Staff reported about the situation in the East. Every report of impending disaster was met with charges of cowardice and treason on the part of the messenger. Besides, the Fuehrer had already committed whatever troops he might have been able to use as reserves in the East to the Ardennes Offensive in the West.

The responsibility for the safety of the German citizens in Warthegau and the other eastern provinces rested not with the military commanders but with civilian governors. These Nazi Party officials, who had control over their own local troops, distrusted the Wehrmacht and saw any military interference in their affairs as a threat. Besides, they often fanatically believed the propaganda from Berlin and in any case weren't going to jeopardize their political power by ordering a "cowardly" evacuation.

In the end, the order to evacuate the Warthegau region wasn't issued until January 21—a full nine days after the front had been shattered. By then over half of the district had already been overrun and hundreds of thousands of refugees were clogging the frozen roads during the worst winter in memory.

Their survival depended almost entirely on chance. Some survived because they were lucky enough to be part of an organized group that was given transportation by retreating German army troops. Others perished because they were in military transports, while those who'd been scheduled to be part of the same group survived only because they'd been left behind and were forced to flee westward on foot. In the chaos of blizzards, airborne bombardment, strafing, and infantry skirmishes, brothers and sisters, mothers and their children became separated, some escaping and some perishing in the snow, and others captured by the Soviets. Horses dropped in their traces for lack of fodder, leaving the roads blocked with their frozen corpses, sleds and wagons. Babies froze to death in their mothers' arms. Mothers froze to death and their still-living infants were taken up and carried by frostbitten strangers.

The Red Army troops, on German soil at last, gave in to unrestrained murder, rape, robbery and looting. The sober reports of what happened to the people living in the villages and towns of the eastern provinces read like bald-faced propaganda. But the fantastic horrors and cruelties are too numerous and consistent and come from too many places and too many reliable witnesses to be discounted.

Women of all ages, ranging from grammar school children to octogenarians, were routinely gang-raped—often to death and sometimes even after they'd died. Many women, in many towns, were crucified, their hands and feet nailed to barn doors or wagons, and then raped and left to die. Fathers and brothers were forced to watch as their wives, mothers, daughters, and sisters were repeatedly sodomized by drunken soldiers before they themselves were executed. Genital mutilation of both men and women occurred frequently, both prior to their deaths and after they'd died.

Unarmed noncombatants of all ages and both sexes were tortured and randomly shot without provocation. Entire villages, captured intact, were left in ashes. The madness often continued for weeks after the initial occupation, with each successive army unit that passed through taking up where their predecessors had left off. In the succeeding months, homes and factories and shops were systematically plundered and dismantled with the spoils loaded onto freight trains for shipment to the Soviet Union.

The Soviet troops had been deliberately fed intense anti-German propaganda for months before the final offensive. They were urged to commit atrocities against German civilians and promised the women as their reward. Many of the Soviet troops were peasants from Siberia and the Soviet Central Asian Republics—Kalmuks, Kazakhs, and Turkmenistani herdsmen from remote villages on the steppes, Islamic and shamanistic peoples with no love of Europeans.

The rape and pillage of these regions was unrestrained not due to a breakdown of discipline, but as part of a Soviet policy aimed at preparing for the post-war shifting of Poland's borders. Under the Yalta agreement, Stalin's troops were to occupy Eastern Europe and Eastern Germany while the Soviet-dominated provisional governments became established and gradually took control over their own nations.

But Stalin had no plans to relinquish control. Instead, he intended to annex the eastern sections of Poland and move the country's borders one hundred miles or so westward into German territory. Before handing the German lands over to a Polish government, the Soviet government deliberately depopulated the area through murder, putting the people to flight, and by mass deportations to the gulags of Siberia. Everything in the way of property that wasn't nailed down (and a good deal of what was nailed down) was shipped to the USSR before handing the despoiled lands over to the Poles.

Roughly 30,000 of the 300,000 Black Sea German civilians who'd survived the trek from Ukraine to Germany died at the hands of Soviet and Allied troops in the months between January and May of 1945. Thousands of the victims were in Dresden awaiting refugee trains on the night of February 13 when American and British bomber squadrons dropped 650,000 incendiary bombs on the city, unleashing a firestorm more immediately destructive than the damage caused by either of the atomic bombings of Hiroshima or Nagasaki.

No one knows just how many of the 68,000 people who died in that raid were German-Russians from Ukraine and Bessarabia. It's impossible to say. Very few of the corpses were identified in the hurried mass burials. A large percentage of the victims were never found or found only as charred pieces of people. Even the estimated total of 68,000 dead is based only on the number of human heads that were found lying in the debris. It is certain that these included many German-Russians, both refugees and soldiers, and likely that at least some of the U.S. Army Air Corps personnel aboard those bombers were American-born German-Russian draftees.

Altogether, eight Heilmann members of the clan served in the German military during the war and seven Heilman members served with the United States and Canada. Only one of the Old World Heilmanns is known to have survived the war; only one of the North American Heilmans died in the war. Those men likely represented about half of the descendants of Johann-Georg and Elisabeth Heilmann who soldiered, since there were, of course, many more cousins who came from the families of their daughters, granddaughters and great-granddaughters.

The Wehrmacht troops on the Eastern front knew full well that their situation was hopeless. By and large, the average soldier, a least among the regular army troops (though not the SS units), fought and died as anti-communists more than as Nazi sympathizers. For the German-Russian draftees like my father's third cousin, Mathias Heilmann, who was killed in December 1944, at Krakow, this was especially so. They'd lived under Soviet rule for twenty-six years and had no illusions about what lay in store for them and their families if they were captured and left to Stalin's mercy.

With the front shattered, rumors began to circulate of a secret peace agreement about to be reached, which would allow the Wehrmacht to fight alongside the Western Allies against the Soviet Union. At the very least, they hoped to slow the Soviet advance long enough for themselves, and especially their families, to escape westward into the hands of the Americans, British and French.

As it turned out, their worst fears were more than justified and their hopes slimmer than they'd thought. Nearly all of the German-Russian Wehrmacht draftees died in battle or were captured by the Soviet troops. The Americans reached the Elbe River and waited on the west side for the Red Army. The Americans and their allies often refused to accept the surrender of German troops who'd fought their way westward to their lines, leaving them to be captured by the Soviets.

As for the families of German-Russian soldiers, despite the horrors of the war, more of their parents, wives and children died as a result of the peace agreements than from the Soviet offensive itself. Roughly 30,000 of the German-Russian refugees were killed by the Soviets, another 180,000 or so were captured in the eastern zone and sent to the gulags of Siberia and Soviet Central Asia.

About 100,000 of them managed to reach the American, British and French occupational zones in the west. About half of these temporarily fortunate ones were arrested there by the Western Allies and handed over to the Soviet government and they too were loaded onto railway cattle cars for the long journey east. "Operation Keelhaul" was the code name given to this round-up of former Soviet citizens by the U.S. Army.

Poorly clothed, underfed and packed together in the "red cow" open cattle cars, the refugees spent eight to twelve weeks on the railroad journey from Occupied Germany to the labor camps in Siberia and Central Asia. About twenty-five percent of them died on the way east, amounting to roughly 46,000 deaths in transit among the Black Sea German-Russians alone during the summer of 1945—over half again as many deaths among these people in the first six months of peace as had died during the final four months of the Soviet offensive itself.

Children of Death

There, in Siberia and Soviet Central Asia, the dying continued. On their arrival all of the men aged sixteen and older were separated from their families and sent to labor camps where they joined captured German soldiers, Russian soldiers who'd been freed from German POW camps and other "enemies of the state." Nine out of every ten of those men died in the camps without ever seeing their families again.

Nor were the women and children spared. The conditions in the women's camps were little better than they were for the men. The work was brutal, the food was inadequate, and the crowded barracks were unsanitary. Malnutrition and contagious diseases claimed their lives by the unknown thousands.

Grandpa's Farm

An' guti Pferd isch seines Futters wert.
A good horse is worth his fodder.

During the 1950s and early 1960s Dad drove to North Dakota every year with Mom in a car full of kids. Two of Mom's brothers had farms near Amidon and Grandpa Heilmann and Dad's sister's husband, Henry Sabo, both farmed near Dickinson. We would leave Los Angeles in the evening for a fourteen hundred-mile drive straight through. It was all two-lane highway back then and the trip took thirty-six hours to pass through Nevada, Utah, Wyoming and South Dakota. Dad smoked cigars the whole way and in the dark coffee-thermos hours after midnight he would sometimes sing old songs from the 1940s such as "She's got pimples on her but she's nice."

By the 1950s Lorenz Heilmann owned 840 acres of farmland a few miles east of Dickinson near the Green River. He farmed mostly wheat for sale and field corn for silage but it was still an old fashioned place with a small multi-breed herd of dairy cows that provided cream for the creamery and milk for the hogs, and beef cattle branded with a Lazy J. The hogs were fed crib corn—ears dried on the cob—which they crunched loudly in a way that frightened me as a small child who had been warned never to set foot in their pen.

It was a lively place, crawling with chickens and geese and half-wild barn cats and patrolled by an elderly swaybacked white horse named Fly, the last of what was once a herd. Lorenz was fond of horses, having learned to handle them in his youth in Czarist Russia. He drove teams as a coal delivery man for a while during World War I and farmed with them all during the 1920s and thirties. It wasn't until World War II that he owned a tractor and, even then, he preferred to send one of his sons out to the fields aboard the machine while he farmed with a team.

He was not alone in clinging to his old ways. His brother-in-law, Jacob Koffler, once stopped by my grandfather J. P. Holzemer's homestead in Amidon and was shown a new tractor. My mother's dad was a great believer in modern farming practices, often the first among his neighbors to try out some new or improved equipment. Jacob looked it over and gave his opinion. "Ah, but, J.P.," he said, "those things don't have no little ones."

During our visits one of my older brothers would ride, half-asleep, out to the pasture in the mornings to bring in the milk cows. It wasn't a difficult task and perhaps not even necessary. The farm's dog would find the cows easily and head them in, and the horse followed the dog while my brother sat riding bareback.

Fly, by the time I knew him, was rumored to be ancient, his age somewhere north of twenty-five years. He moved slowly, plodding along resignedly with three or four kids on his broad back when we rode him to the Green River ford down the road from the farm.

Fly finally went lame in 1959. That was the same year that Grandpa later had a stroke and retired from farming, sold the place and moved into town. I remember my father talking about how his dad had walked alongside the old horse from the farm to the stock-auction house on the edge of Dickinson where Fly was sold to a rendering plant's buyer. I can't think back on it without sadness. In my mind I see that old farmer in his bib overalls at the end of his way of life leading the last of his horses to auction.

Courtyard

*Sauf dich voll und fress dich dick
Aber halt dich weg von der Politik.*

Drink yourself full and eat yourself fat
But stay away from politics.

The BBC News brought me bad news from Kandel, Rheinland-Pfalz. As the program ran footage of protest marches and counter-marches, I learned that a young girl, age fifteen, had been murdered by an immigrant. Here, in my small Oregon town, some people speak of the danger of allowing immigrants to settle among us. There, in the place where my ancestors lived so long ago, the same fear walks the streets.

I watched in dismay, saddened by memories from an evening in Kandel some twenty-two years before.

The restaurant was recommended to me as a place to try an old-fashioned Pfalzer meal. Sitting in the courtyard of an old building in Kandel that dates back to the mid-eighteenth century, I dined on pork cutlets, potatoes, bread, and a liter of cloudy Hefeweissen beer. It was a lovely little spot with whitewashed walls and a grape arbor overhead, green with new leaves on the vines. The evening light was softening and the food was quite good. Looking around, it occurred to me that my great-great-great grandfather undoubtedly knew this building and perhaps sat in this same space nearly two hundred years ago.

The place was not crowded. A small family was eating supper to my left and a few tables away to my right, five middle-aged men were gathered carrying on an animated conversation that I didn't understand because I hadn't enough of my own ancestral language to make out more than a word here or there. Still, the men in their suits were a familiar grouping, business men by the looks of them, the sort of people who, at home, attend Chamber of Commerce luncheons and complain about their taxes.

Eavesdropping is my lifelong habit and despite not understanding more than one word in every eight, I couldn't help but listen to them. Their tone was enough to let me know the drift of their conversation. They were not happy about whatever it was that they were talking about, whether it was politics or government regulation or some other way in which everything seemed to be going straight to hell lately.

Then I caught two words, *Russland* and *aussiedleren*. They were talking, it seemed, about ethnic German immigrants from Russia, over a million of whom had arrived in the recently reunited Germany. They were not happy about it. And a desire to approach them and to question them to learn their thoughts grew in me.

A few days before this I'd met with the mayor of Germersheim, the district capital, and learned of the city government's efforts to assimilate these immigrants.

Cut off for generations from their ethnic culture and from western European democracy, they required a good deal of housing and income support as well as special classes in order to settle in their ancestral homeland. And this came at a time when Germany was also busy working to deal with reunification with the eastern portion of the nation.

I'd met some of the German-Russian immigrants, seen the anti-immigrant graffiti sprayed on the sides of railcars. A Greek waiter in Kandel had told me of the distaste that many local people have expressed for foreign workers. A reporter in Kaiserlautern spoke of the rise of neo-nazi skinhead groups in the country.

I was overwhelmed by a desire to join the men at their table and ask them questions. But the fact remained that I would not have been able to understand the answers to the poorly phrased questions I'd have asked these men. Merely being understood when you clumsily speak is difficult and daunting enough.

There was, I realized, nothing I could do in this situation, except to wonder about what I was missing out on and to regret, once again, knowing so little.

I kept to myself until the waitress approached my table and asked the universal waitress question near the end of a meal. I summoned up a few German phrases in answer, *"S'isch genung. Die rechnung bitter"*—"It is enough. The reckoning please."

By the same author:
OVERSTORY: ZERO
REAL LIFE IN TIMBER COUNTRY
2nd Edition

Robert Leo Heilman's award-winning essay collection about work, family, community, and the land is back in print, revised and expanded with ten new pieces added about small-town life in timber country.

Sylph Maid Books

P.O. Box 932
Myrtle Creek, OR 97457 U.S.A.

Phone: (541) 863-5069

By the same author:

THE WORLD POOL
A LITERARY VARIETY

The World Pool is an eclectic collection of short works selected from the author's thirty years' worth of freelance writing, 1985-2015. This literary variety show brings readers a swirl of essays, articles, vignettes and short stories that range across the personal, historical and fanciful worlds of life. Here's your chance to jump aboard this merry-go-round of thoughts and stories for a brief tour through so much of what it means to be human.

Sylph Maid Books

P.O. Box 932
Myrtle Creek, OR 97457 U.S.A.

Phone: (541) 863-5069

www.ingramcontent.com/pod-product-compliance
Lightning Source LLC
Chambersburg PA
CBHW020422010526
44118CB00010B/379